Praise for

HEALTHY IS THE NEW SKINNY

"**Katie Willcox**'s personality and her passion for healthy body image resonate throughout this entire book. Her message is both powerful and relatable. I feel that <u>Healthy Is the New Skinny</u> can be every girl's go-to guide for empowerment and body positivity!"

— **Robyn Lawley**, international supermodel, designer, and author of *Robyn Lawley Eats*

"*A lively and useful guide to understanding and overcoming the destructive messages of the beauty ideal.* **Katie Willcox** *shares her journey with wisdom, insight, and humor, encouraging us to love our bodies and reclaim our power—not just to improve our own lives but also, more importantly, to change the world.*"

— **Jean Kilbourne, Ed.D.**, activist, speaker, creator of the film series *Killing Us Softly: Advertising's Image of Women*, and author of *Can't Buy My Love: How Advertising Changes the Way We Think and Feel*

"**Katie Willcox** is such a positive voice for balance, wellness, and radiant self-confidence in the online world and modeling industry. Now, with this book, I am thrilled that she will be able to reach even more people with her message. (YES for 'girl gangs'!) I can absolutely relate to the struggle to find inner confidence that Katie writes so thoughtfully about—and, man, all I can say is that once you do find it, incredible things happen! Katie tells her story with such beauty and eloquence that, after reading this book, I feel like we are the best of friends."

— **Jordan Younger**, founder of The Balanced Blonde and author of *Breaking Vegan*

"**Katie Willcox**'s altruistic personality and first-hand experience in the modeling industry come through in this book to cultivate a welcoming, positive, and insightful environment for women of all ages to feel empowered."

— **John Edward**, psychic medium, author, and host of *Crossing Over with John Edward* and *Evolve with John Edward*

HEALTHY
is the new SKINNY

HEALTHY

is the new SKINNY

YOUR GUIDE TO SELF-LOVE
IN A "PICTURE PERFECT" WORLD

KATIE H. WILLCOX

HAY HOUSE, INC.
Carlsbad, California • New York City
London • Sydney • Johannesburg
Vancouver • New Delhi

Published and distributed in the United States by: Hay House, Inc.: www .hayhouse.com® • *Published and distributed in Australia by:* Hay House Australia Pty. Ltd.: www.hayhouse.com.au • *Published and distributed in the United Kingdom by:* Hay House UK, Ltd.: www.hayhouse.co.uk • *Published and distributed in the Republic of South Africa by:* Hay House SA (Pty), Ltd.: www.hayhouse.co.za • *Distributed in Canada by:* Raincoast Books: www.raincoast.com • *Published in India by:* Hay House Publishers India: www.hayhouse.co.in

Editor: Brookes Nohlgren, www.booksbybrookes.com
Project editor: Nicolette Salamanca Young
Cover design: Jessica Brittell
Interior design: Pamela Homan

Library of Congress Cataloging-in-Publication Data

Names: Willcox, Katie H., date, author.
Title: Healthy is the new skinny : your guide to self-love in a "picture perfect" world / Katie H. Willcox.
Description: 1st edition. | Carlsbad, California : Hay House, Inc., [2017]
Identifiers: LCCN 2016037602 | ISBN 9781401947217 (tradepaper : alk. paper)
Subjects: LCSH: Body image in women. | Self-acceptance. | Self-esteem.
Classification: LCC BF697.5.B63 W5495 2017 | DDC 306.4/613--dc23 LC record available at https://lccn.loc.gov/2016037602

ISBN: 978-1-4019-4721-7

10 9 8 7 6 5 4 3 2 1
1st edition, January 2017

Printed in the United States of America

THIS BOOK IS
DEDICATED TO MY MOTHER,
JANICE WHITE, AND TO MY HUSBAND,
BRADFORD WILLCOX; OUR BABY GIRL, TRUE;
AND OUR PIT BULL, ATHENA. TOGETHER, AS
A FAMILY, WE WILL BREAK THE GENERATIONAL
MESSAGING THAT TELLS LITTLE GIRLS THEY ARE NOT
GOOD ENOUGH. INSTEAD, WE WILL RAISE TRUE
IN AN ENVIRONMENT THAT PROTECTS AND
SUPPORTS HER UNIQUE SENSE OF
SELF, WHICH WILL ALWAYS BE
LOVED AND ACCEPTED.

Contents

A Note from the Author

I know what you might be thinking . . . "Oh, another book by a model telling me to love myself exactly as I am. Easy for her to say! I'm sure it's easy to feel beautiful inside when you're *also* beautiful on the outside!" And I'm not saying your eye roll isn't justified. That is the world we live in. A world where looks are everything, and we are judged and valued based on how closely we match our society's beauty ideal.

Well, I'd like to show you where society has gone wrong, how we have bought into a collective belief that is astonishingly untrue, how it *is* possible to love yourself—truly—exactly as you are right now, and why that is actually the best possible thing you could do . . . for yourself and for the world.

Hear me out. I promise not to patronize you or tell you anything that I don't believe is 100 percent true. I have been on both sides of the beauty fence. Over the course of my 30 short years, I have both worked as a professional model and been the exact opposite of our culture's ideal of what is beautiful. I, too, have struggled with my weight. I have been on the seesaw of gaining and shedding dozens and dozens of pounds. As I describe it, I have been the "big girl in a skinny world," feeling like I didn't and never would fit in.

Then I had a powerful realization: I was miserable no matter which end of the weight spectrum I was on. My self-loathing didn't change with my weight or how "pretty" society thought I was, so my looks weren't the source of happiness and self-worth that I had believed them to be. But if it wasn't my looks, then what was it? And, equally important, how had I come to invest so much of myself in a belief that was so untrue? How had I gotten so far off track?

Finding the answers to these and related questions has been the greatest journey of my life so far. It has caused a complete turnaround in my level of happiness and sense of self-worth. In these pages, I share that journey and the lessons I learned along the way so that you, too, may learn to love yourself exactly the way you are right now and set yourself free from the cage you are currently imprisoned in.

You are meant for great things in this world. It's time you realized it. May this book be a step on your journey to that greatness.

■ ■ ■ ■ ■

Introduction

I'm not here to sell you a glamorized image of the fashion industry or pump you with contradictory messages like so many women's magazines today. I didn't write this book to promote my career as a model or share my "beauty secrets" with you. We won't be talking about diets, carbs, calories, or the "dos and don'ts" of health. You won't find any tips about makeup, makeovers, or exercise routines. I wrote this book because I have something to say about the culture we live in; the beauty ideal that is keeping girls and women small; and the world of false advertising that has hijacked our self-image, health, happiness, beauty, and value, leaving our souls starving for meaning and purpose.

We live in a culture that teaches girls and women that our value comes from our bodies, and that we must keep those bodies small. It's no wonder that many of us have developed a love/hate relationship with food. While you may not consider yourself to have an eating disorder, the truth is that when it comes to our collective relationship with food, we clearly have some issues. After all, how many women and girls do you know who constantly think or talk about food? How many have a sense of guilt, shame, or self-loathing based on what they eat? How many eat for comfort or out of anxiety?

How many of your friends and family members have gone from one extreme form of eating to another? A beauty ideal has been created that is abnormally thin, leading to a culture of disordered eating in generations of girls and women in pursuit of acceptance, value, and love. I want us to talk about that, and that's exactly what we will explore in this book. This book is based on my experience of being a woman searching for my true beauty in this "picture perfect" culture and world.

And let me tell you, that is no easy task. Although statistics abound, I don't need Harvard to tell me that the world views and treats females as secondary. I see women's second-class status in the way that the basic human rights of so many women around the world are denied. I see it in the double standard women face when it comes to sexuality, where men are praised for being sexually active as a symbol of manhood while women are looked down on for the same behavior. I see it in the lack of women in leadership and managerial positions, and unequal wages between men and women for the same work.

These issues are nothing new. For generations, there have been women who have dedicated their lives to achieving equality and a better world for all. These women were warriors who were brave enough not to follow the crowd or acquiesce to the institutions that were causing girls and women harm. They stood up and sometimes stood alone to fight for others and themselves. To do so, they had to leave fear behind and go on a journey to discover their true selves, their life purpose, and the inevitable truth that the validation they sought from others actually must come from within. I have chosen to be one of these women, and you can, too! I am not simply a model. I am a woman who is becoming aware and conscious. As a result, I'm not willing to turn a blind eye and allow life to continue the way it has been.

As a young girl, I can remember being so consumed with anxiety about my body and how I looked. I worried what other people said about me and if they liked me. I thought for sure no boys would ever like me because I was just too fat. I was so consumed with these negative thoughts about how the outside world perceived me that I never stopped to think for myself and ask the most important question: Why?

Why does everyone want me to be something other than who and what I am? Why don't I know any women who like how they look? Why do I always feel as if I am never enough? Why does my 85-year-old grandmother incessantly ask, "Does my hair look okay?" I don't know about you, but to this day, I have never looked at an 85-year-old woman and critiqued her hair, yet Gramma is sure that this is the topic of conversation no matter where we go. *Why?*

To find the answers to these and related questions, I went on my own journey for the truth, and what I discovered changed my life. The beautiful thing about asking questions is that when you ask one, every answer you find, every realization, leads you to the next important question. Somewhere along the road of my awakening process, I realized that I had to decide what kind of woman I was going to be. Was I going to be someone who looked good on the outside and followed the path that was expected of her, always working to please others? Was I willing to live with and try to live up to the standards set by society in an attempt to feel appreciated and of value? Or was I courageously going to turn away from that well-worn path and walk into the unknown without a map dictating where I should go?

I decided that if I was going to live an authentic life that didn't just look good but actually *felt good in my soul*, I had to leave behind the beliefs others had passed on to me. I had to let go of ideas, dreams, and programming that had never belonged to me in the first place. I had to go back to square one, nothingness, zero. Only then could I discover what was right for me and would make me happy.

So I did. I turned my back on the path I had been traveling down and walked away from a life that always left me feeling empty. I realized that my dream of being a top model came from a desire to feel as if I have value. I wanted a chance to make a difference in the world. Modeling would never give me that, so I would have to discover what would. I bravely and blindly set out into a new, foreign landscape with nothing but the heavens and my own inner compass as my guide.

Along the way, I founded my own agency, Natural Model Management (NMM). While it might seem ironic that I would create a modeling agency, I realized that one of the best ways to fight the portrayal of unhealthy bodies in the media is to make sure there are more realistic, natural, healthy models out there. NMM doesn't focus on traditional "plus-size" or "straight-size" models (you'll learn more about these designations in Chapter 2). Our mission is to let models be healthy and happy, while providing them with an opportunity to work as models at their natural body shapes and sizes.

I've also founded the company Healthy Is the New Skinny (HNS). It started as a simple personal blog but has since transformed into a social movement for healthy body image and female empowerment. Through social-media outreach and Re-Model Me workshops, we show young girls and women the effect the media has on their body image and self-esteem, and challenge the views they have of themselves and their bodies.

Now I am blessed to say that I know who I am, what I believe, and why I am here. I've created two successful businesses, an amazing and loving marriage with my soul mate, and a fierce connection to my soul and purpose in life. I have found tremendous peace and joy, and I know I made the right decision all those years ago to question everything I thought I knew.

One little word will be the game changer of your life: "Why?" For example, when I challenged what I had been taught about beauty and what it should mean to me, it led me to eye-opening discoveries about the beauty industry. When I traveled to other countries and met people I really liked, it challenged my beliefs about the natural superiority of any nationality or spirituality. When I questioned why I was here on this planet, I found answers that revealed my life purpose and subsequently led me here, to you.

By sharing my journey into myself, I hope to inspire you to make a similar pilgrimage. That is the purpose of this book, which is arranged as follows: In Part I, I shed some light on what may be your dream right now: to be a model or just look like one. We take a close look at the Western beauty ideal, where it originated, and why its purpose is to be unattainable. We ask important questions like, "Who are we trying to be beautiful for?" In Part II, I give you information and exercises to help you take your power back in a healthy way. We work to break your negative thinking so you can make the shift from self-loathing to self-love. I teach you why "healthy is the new skinny" and how redefining beauty gives you the opportunity to create a new relationship with your body. Part III is all about getting started being you—the real you, that is. When you discover who you really are as a person, you allow yourself the opportunity to find your life purpose and passion. I show you how! Last, in Part IV, we look at how we can use all this knowledge, freedom, and power to make a positive difference in the world together.

I hope you will go on this journey with me to challenge your own beliefs about life, the world, beauty, relationships, goals, family, dreams, and even your own identity. It's not easy, but when you allow yourself to start over with your beliefs and programming, you grant yourself permission to not only exist but to really live! Because when you start from nothing, there is nothing but the opportunity for expansion and growth. You can discover and consciously create who you were born to become.

Let's get started!

■ ■ ■ ■ ■

Part One

WHY WE FEEL BAD ABOUT OURSELVES

Chapter 1

A False Dream

I have almost 15 years of experience as a model, and 5 years of experience being a modeling agency owner and CEO. I have 12 years of experience being an overweight, outspoken, freethinking, school-hating kid. Total, I have 30 years of experience being a girl, woman, and human being.

I have traveled to many high schools and colleges to give Re-Model Me presentations on media manipulation and body image—some of the topics we cover in this book. During these workshops, I share candidly how my experiences as a model were not fulfilling to my soul and how that led me on a journey to discover who I really was and what I wanted for my life beyond being viewed as beautiful by others, how my drive for change propelled me into creating two successful businesses by the age of 25. I describe how I lost 40 pounds and in the process discovered what real "health" meant to me, and how today I preach words of female empowerment and self-love to help women of all ages return to an intimate relationship with their true selves. After every event, groups of girls wait to speak with me. While they start out by saying, "I was so inspired by everything you said," the conversation always turns to "How do *I* become a model?"

The Question Girls Ask Me

I have learned so much about how girls think from these encounters. Hand in hand with their question about how to become a model, they also open up about their emotional struggles with how they perceive their own bodies. Sadly, self-loathing is the dominant theme. Their feelings are fresh and raw. As much as they might tell me how inspired they were, the words they use reveal to me that they still hold the belief that modeling is the key to having the life they want, that being a model is the answer to that deep sense of insecurity, self-loathing, and unhappiness they tell me they feel.

This wasn't just happening at my presentations. Many girls and women have reached out to me online, as I have fairly large Instagram and Facebook presences. I share body-image and health inspiration and post content that challenges our societal view of beauty and health. I post everything from amazing quotes and daily thoughts to funny things we can all relate to as women, healthy recipes that look and taste amazing, and (my personal favorite) inspiring stories from other women. It is important to me to showcase a wide variety of body types to accurately depict what health and wellness really look like.

Women from around the world have joined our social-media movement. (Most of the members of my community are girls and women ages 13 to 30 on Instagram, and 25 and up on Facebook.) They'll post photos of themselves with our products, often working out and giving a positive message to other women who are striving to bring health and wellness into their everyday lives. Yet, despite all the body-positive images and messaging I post, I was being asked the same question repeatedly by my followers.

The Truth about Being a Role Model and the Misguided Search for Value

One girl, a 15-year-old from Mississippi, wrote to me, asking, "How can I be a model?" Seeing this as a great opportunity to find out what was driving her and other girls' desire to be a model, I asked her, "Why do you want to be a model?"

"I want to be a role model for girls and show that all bodies are beautiful," she said. My initial thought when someone tells they want to be a "role model" is that they have misinterpreted the meaning, the same way I once did. Rather than desiring to live an inspiring life that others want to model their own after, oftentimes people associate "role model" with simply being famous. They desire to be a role model as a means of gaining mass acceptance and validation.

I responded, "I admire that you want to inspire girls and women to love who they are, but can I ask you why you think that is connected to modeling? Models help companies sell clothing and other products and services. You are correct in that what you are describing is a role model, but it's not a model. The two are very different things!"

Her reply revealed what many girls believe: "No one cares what I have to say, but if I were a model, I would have a lot of followers and people would listen to me." On one level, of course, she is right! Because our current social-media platforms are image driven, models do have an advantage creating an audience. However, for many models, most of the social-media audience is made up of male followers who lust after their images. The rest of the audience is generally made up of girls and women who want to emulate the images. I think it is important to realize that it is not the size of the audience that matters when promoting important societal issues; rather, it is the type of audience you build and the influence you can have, both of which transcend what looks alone can generate.

After reading thousands of e-mails and messages on Facebook and Instagram, it has become clear to me that far too many young girls fall prey to the notion that being a model, actress, or pop star is the only way they can feel valued and important, or even be heard. While it's easy to think that if you were a model, then people would care what you have to say, it's just not accurate. Oftentimes women who are beautiful are stereotyped as stupid and not taken seriously. Every single woman has different barriers to overcome, just like we all have different talents and gifts to offer.

What Does It Take to Become a Model?

When I opened Natural Model Management (NMM) in 2011, I took a giant leap of faith, left my representation at the top agency in the industry, and started to represent myself. My goal was to empower myself and other models to have a healthy experience in the industry and, with any luck, do what I could to actually transform the industry for the better from the inside out. When we started, I was the only model we represented. But for NMM to succeed as a business, I also had to find other models, fast!

We would scout girls all over the place, looking for those who matched our criteria. Our agency represents what the industry considers "plus-size" models. At NMM, we prefer to call our girls "curve" models because we feel the term *plus-size* is a misnomer—the majority of them are not plus-size by society's view. They are just normal-size women, albeit well above average height. Our models range from five eight to six feet and sizes 8 to 18. Once we found them, we then gave the girls nicknames based on where we met them: Suzie was "Target" because we scouted her while in line at the checkout. Tara was "Chili's" because we saw her at dinner one evening. As our board of models grew, we started to receive online submissions.

It was so interesting to see who would submit photos to us and why. It wasn't just one type of person who would contact us in the hopes of becoming a model. We would get young, old, big, small, round, short, tall—all shapes and sizes you could imagine. The ones that bothered us the most were the photos of naked babies. Yes, people send photos of their naked babies and even children to modeling agencies!

Although we stated clearly on our website what we were looking for and the types of photos to submit, it didn't seem to deter hundreds of people from sending in photos that didn't fit the criteria. After a while, I started to wonder about what drove some of these people. For example, what would compel a 45-year-old mother of four to submit photos to try to begin a modeling career at that stage in her life? Of course, a woman who is 45 and a mother can have stunning physical beauty and be very photogenic, but models typically begin their careers in their teenage years. If they are good at what they do and can meet and maintain the body size requirements, they can have a relatively long career. But the fact is that it's not something one can usually start in midlife. Like anything you want to be good at, it takes time and development; it takes many years and a lot of hard work and sacrifice to have a thriving career. Yet the general perception of modeling is that this isn't the case.

When it comes to modeling, there is a belief that it's something you can just say, "Hey, I want to do this," and that's it. No one thinks about the years of learning the business and becoming good at it. I have worked professionally as a model for so long it has become something I can do in my sleep, but it took more than 15 years for me to get to this place. The work and struggle involved in modeling isn't portrayed in the media, when it's discussed at all.

The truth is that the modeling industry is shrouded in a bit of mystery. In fact, its mystery was the driving force behind the success of the TV show *America's Next Top Model* and local model searches. However, the information spread on those two platforms is very misleading. As a TV show, *America's Next Top Model* is produced to be entertaining to viewers, not to be an accurate depiction of the modeling industry. Small-town model searches often manipulate people into buying services they don't need or paying to be seen by agents, which anyone can do for free. I don't believe the lack of information available to the public is intentional; I just feel that the industry is similar to an onion, with many layers to peel back and understand.

Even if you try to research modeling, you won't find much information online. You'll find short, behind-the-scenes marketing videos that companies display on their websites, with fast clips of girls laughing, getting glammed up, and taking pictures to cool, upbeat music. It makes modeling look incredibly hip, carefree, and fun—like something any young girl should desire to do. You will find all kinds of websites and model searches ready to take your money, telling you that they will assist you in becoming a model. But, again, what does that mean? How does it work? What does it require? No one really knows the true reality of it except for the people inside the industry.

A Dream of Specialness

I have asked myself, "If none of the people who desire to be models have any experience or knowledge about the industry or the profession of modeling, how could becoming a model really be an authentic dream for them?" This can be said of any career, but the danger is that there is no honest depiction of modeling and no way to gain experience or education before pursuing it. Some young women have the skills and luck necessary to launch a career, but many others do not. Yet so many young girls seem to have the same fervent "dream" of being a model, even before they know anything about the reality. Why is that?

To understand this better, I asked the question of myself. Why did *I* want to be a model when I had never tried it before, having no idea if I would be good at it or if I would find it enjoyable or fulfilling? I'd never given it any consideration; I'd simply had this "dream." Sure, as I developed and grew, I ended up naturally having many of the features that allowed me to meet the criteria required for one small segment of the modeling industry. But that doesn't explain why I had wanted to be a model much, much earlier than that, when I looked the opposite of what models were. So, why did I? To find out, I had to backtrack a bit and look at how the dream had evolved for me.

As I share more about in Chapter 6, the first I learned of modeling was when I was nine and a model search came through town. My two beautiful, petite cousins went to it and were selected, while I—who looked just about as different from them as I possibly could—was left at home. My mother and aunts were trying to protect my feelings, because everyone knew there was no way I would be chosen. Still, the idea of becoming a model and that association with being "special" was planted and would continue to pull at me on and off over the years.

Throughout most of my youth, I wasn't considered beautiful like my cousins were. I also wasn't particularly feminine the way models are. In fact, in junior high I was given the nickname "The Beast," because of my specialty in a basketball play called a "screen." I would act as a wall of sorts for the point guard to lead the other team's defender into. (The defender unknowingly slams into the screen instead of continuing to guard their opponent, which sets the point guard free to make a play.) Girls would run into me at full speed, often injuring themselves, while I wouldn't budge an inch. It was as if they had run into a brick wall. Not very model-like!

But then in the ninth grade, a random event occurred that reignited my model dream. A girl came up to me at school one day and said, "We were looking at a magazine last night, and there is a girl in it that looks just like you!" I remember that moment vividly, because it stunned me. I wasn't sure what she meant exactly, but her comment made me feel special. No one had ever complimented my looks. Yes, I'd had a few really strange backhanded comments from older people, like one lady who said, "You are so beautiful; you remind me of Shamu." I thought, *Did this lady really just tell me I remind her of a whale? Yes, she did!* She did go on to explain that it was because my skin was "so beautiful and flawless," but the damage had been done. At that point, I had not perceived myself as attractive at all, so to have a girl come up and say I looked like a model was definitely unexpected.

Then, in my junior year of high school, I began to really daydream about modeling. *America's Next Top Model* was a hit show, and watching it somehow sparked the idea that maybe, just maybe, I could do it. The show would take normal-looking girls and transform them into "top models" (with, of course, the help of liberal amounts of Photoshop). Regardless, the effect on most girls, including me, was, "I am just a normal girl—maybe I can be a top model, too!" The girls on the show were clearly getting to do amazing things, and their lives looked way better than mine. If you asked me then why I wanted to model, I would have said something similar to what girls say to me today: "Because it looks fun." "I want to travel." "I love taking pictures." "I want to be a role model for girls." That all makes sense on the surface, but today I realize that the real reason was something else.

It wasn't fun or excitement or adventure I wanted; it was acceptance. I was drawn to the idea of being chosen for something portrayed as "special." *I* wanted to be special! I was never the one chosen, not ever; even as a child, I'd been left out of the model search. I think that feeling is common among girls. I always felt that I was meant to do something important in life, and because of models' perceived value in our culture, becoming one seemed like a way to achieve that. It's the reason girls ask me the question via e-mail, Facebook, and Instagram. It's the reason they ask me at every presentation I give. It's the reason we get submissions from countless people through our agency website—because the media and our culture tell us we should be models (or at least beautiful and model-like), and then we will be of value. Then we will matter and count. We take the message in without stopping to think about whether it's true.

Vulnerability and Insecurity

At my first modeling shoot, I discovered firsthand that modeling is not as fun and easy as the media often makes it out to be. I walked into the photo studio feeling completely inadequate. I was used to walking down the halls at my high school, not a runway. I had never been to a photo shoot and had no idea what to expect. I walked in and was immediately overwhelmed by the racks upon racks of shoes and clothing. I had never seen anything like it. There were people everywhere, but no one acknowledged me or seemed to notice I was there. I felt really out of place and wondered if maybe I literally *was* in the wrong place! I think I stood there long enough looking lost that I became annoying to some of the crew, and they finally pointed me in the right direction.

The first thing I did was try on some of the outfits I was going to wear that day so the stylist could see how they fit and make adjustments. Next was hair and makeup. I was so excited about getting my hair and makeup done because I had only ever had it done at the mall, and I was sure this was going to be so much better! I sat there for what seemed like ages, and when I finally got to look in the mirror, I turned around full of excitement only to be surprised to see myself looking like . . . well, just me. I was confused. It didn't really look as if I had any makeup on at all, and they left my hair the way it was naturally—straight. I remember feeling a little bummed out because I thought I was going to look like a model, but I didn't think I looked like one at all. I just looked normal.

They called me on set, which consisted of a giant paper backdrop with a piece of tape on the floor to mark where I was to stand. I walked to my mark and just stood there with an awkward smile. There were lights on both sides of me flashing and one behind me. There was a computer screen to the side with my images popping up as the photographer snapped them. There were seven people looking at me and telling me what to do. I was scared shitless. Finally the stylist asked if I was new. I said, "Yes, this is my first photo shoot."

She replied, "Ever? Like, ever, ever?"

"Ever," I said with a smile.

That is when things got a little better for me because she showed me how to pose and move on set. I was able to see and learn as I went along, and I realized that modeling was nothing like I expected it to be. Modeling is more than just a title; it is a real profession with a lot of pressure, expectations, and hard physical work.

The first shoot is terrifying but even more so is seeing your photos for the first time on a website, in store windows, or in newspapers. My first thought when I saw my pictures on that first client's website was, *Ewww, I look terrible.* I hated them! Just like my hair and makeup experience, I was expecting to see a model when I looked at my photos. But I just saw myself, and I thought I looked fat. I thought my arms looked big, and my cheeks were way too chubby. I cringed clicking through them and thought for sure there was no way that company would ever hire me again. To my shock and amazement, they did. As an adult I look back at those photos, and, yes, you can tell I was not as experienced as I am now. But they were by no means ugly or terrible like I had thought. I viewed those images through the eyes of my teenage self, who was hopeful and excited to see something better, more beautiful, and special on the screen. Sadly, my low self-esteem stopped me from seeing what the client saw all along: a beautiful girl looking great in their clothing.

The media has created the belief that if you are a model, then you are beautiful and special, and you will be happy, desirable, successful, and fulfilled. Years after my first shoot, when I finally stopped to think about that more, I realized my *true* dream was not to be a model but rather to have all the values we associate with being one. At the core of it all, I wanted to find validation that *I* was important. The media sold me the idea of being a model as the key to fulfilling that goal.

The False Dream of Modeling

Having lived the "dream" for 15 years, I can report that it does not deliver the promised payoff. The fantasy of becoming a model (or even just looking like one) to feel special is a false dream, and the pursuit of it will leave us feeling short-changed and empty every time. There are a few reasons for this. One is that in the world of modeling, you are always waiting for others to choose you: You need an agency to pick you to be represented. You need art directors to pick you as the model for a brand or magazine. You sit and wait for others to tell you what to do in order to be picked or chosen, and it can be easy to let that same pattern take over your life. You sit in limbo, waiting for someone to recognize you and give you permission to do something or be someone great. This makes us feel powerless over our own destiny, dependent on others for approval and success, and thus fundamentally inept and insecure. While there may be numerous careers where someone is dependent on their services being chosen by a client, it's especially hard when *you* are the product you're trying to sell and rejection is so prevalent.

Compounding that for models is that we're also constantly at the receiving end of others' judgments, opinions, and criticisms about how we look. As I share in upcoming chapters, most models are constantly watched, critiqued, and told to change things about themselves, including their weight. Once I became a model, I spent a long time trying to fit other people's ideas of beauty, both inside and outside the modeling industry. In the industry, I listened when people told me to gain weight so that I could work as a plus-size model; I listened when they told me to cut my hair, get a tan, or dress a specific way. Outside the industry, I listened to people tell me that I would be much more attractive if I lost weight. As a result of listening to what others told me I needed to be, I was left feeling unaccepted for who I was— never quite "good enough" according to some outer ideal. I was left feeling empty, insecure, and unfulfilled. I felt this way for quite a while before actually admitting it to myself.

The desire to be someone great is why girls fantasize about being a model. Yet I realized that constantly having to alter myself to be what others wanted so I would be chosen was never going to allow me to be truly great or successful, because greatness requires authenticity. I realized that before I could become great I had to figure out *who I was*. So I did the only thing I could: I started asking questions I'd never thought to ask before.

I remember the milestone day that, for me, brought all this to a head. I was 19 and flying to Germany for a modeling job when my "model dream" balloon finally burst. As I was looking out the window at a beautiful, snow-covered landscape, I had an epiphany: *This is all bullshit!* Don't get me wrong; I was happy to travel and work, but no matter how much I worked or how many places I went, I felt lost. I felt really alone and had this homesick feeling that wouldn't go away even when I would go home. I experienced a lot of confusion and conflict because I watched *America's Next Top Model* and knew that those girls were all competing for what I had. *So* many girls around the world wanted what I had. I thought *I* wanted what I had!

Yet I felt empty. I discovered that the reality of modeling is not the dream we are sold as young girls. Even though I could officially say, "I am a model"—I was signed with a top agency in New York City and was working and making money—*it didn't fix me.* It didn't make me feel happy, valuable, or fulfilled. It was this state of confusion and inner conflict that caused me to question so many things in my life. As soon as I started to examine my life and ask "Why?" I was forced to take an honest look at myself and the path I was headed down, which ultimately allowed me to change course and discover a new path that led me to a much more fulfilling place.

This is an important piece of wisdom I hope to impart with this book. When we are sold a belief, dream, or idea that is not ours but we accept as our own, we long for, chase, and maybe even achieve the idea, dream, or belief. Yet we never attain the satisfaction or fulfillment we were promised would come with it. That's because whatever we were seeking was not authentic to who we truly are. That dream, idea, or belief that we had accepted as ours was not born from our hearts and souls; it was a program we downloaded from elsewhere and accepted as true. Authentic ideas, dreams, and beliefs do not leave us feeling hollow and empty. They are the spark that keeps us lit up and alive.

In our culture, beauty equals value, and that message is received loud and clear. This belief is so powerful for girls that it has convinced them to starve and alter their bodies; and for far too many, it has restricted their aspirations to a very narrow goal. We have raised generations of girls to spend their lives working to please others and gain acceptance, hoping to one day be "enough." We have taught them to focus on perfecting their bodies—which they have learned is the only thing that counts—in hopes of earning love and being granted permission to be someone great. We have rendered them powerless, worthless, and unlovable as they are so that they can spend their lives purchasing products and diet plans to "fix" themselves and become worthy of being known. We have made them believe they have no value unless they alter who they are to fit the images corporations have created as the female ideal.

■ ■ ■

In the remaining chapters of Part I, I show you why being a model (or wanting to look like one) is not a true dream but rather something we have been manipulated to want by people who profit from our believing that it is. In addition to being a false dream, for nearly all of us it's also unattainable. That's not because we are failures or not good enough, but because that's the way it was designed to be.

■ ■ ■ ■ ■

Chapter 2

An Unattainable Ideal

In Chapter 1, we discussed how the desire to become a model (or just to look like one) is, for nearly every one of us, a false dream—one that does not originate with us, and is programmed into us by the media. It plays into our deep desire to feel special, accepted, valued, and loved. In this chapter, I'd like to show you how our culture's ideal of beauty is unattainable for the majority of us and designed to be that way. Let's examine this ideal that we are being asked to live up to.

Our Unhealthy Image of Beauty

In Chapter 9, we examine how beauty ideals differ around the world, but for now let's examine what is perceived and portrayed as beauty in the United States. I would argue that the following physical features are prized: light skin, above-average height, a perfect complexion, long hair, thinness, a large butt, big boobs, a small waist, full lips, thin legs, thin arms, a small nose, and big eyes. All of those body parts rarely coincide naturally without plastic surgery. Furthermore, we're often comparing our real selves with digitally altered images of celebrities who have had surgery to fit this beauty ideal! Our beauty ideal is one that is not natural to the female body, making it unattainable without altering the body through unnatural means.

Female models represent the beauty ideal in our culture for girls and women. We are raised with the belief that youth and beauty are the sources of our value and importance. Perhaps the most unattainable features of models—if you don't possess them naturally—are extreme thinness and above-average height. "Models have always been skinny and tall," legendary fashion designer Diane von Furstenberg stated, "and that's fine as long as they're healthy." But are they?

Sadly, most female runway models have a body mass index (BMI) consistent with anorexia. BMI is a weight-to-height ratio. According to the World Health Organization, an adult with a BMI below 18.5 is considered underweight; a BMI below 16 indicates being severely thin. A low BMI is associated with certain health risks, such as an impaired immune system, bone loss, iron-deficiency anemia, and cardiac problems. The average model is five nine, weighs 110 pounds, and has a BMI of 16—far below what's healthy.

When i came up with the name "Healthy Is the New Skinny" for a body-image blog I was creating, I wanted to draw attention to the pressure models face in the industry to be ultrathin. In the fashion industry, no matter how small girls are, it seems people are always suggesting that they get smaller to be more successful. That is wrong. If we care about women, the focus should not be on making girls skinnier but instead on being healthy. If the industry allowed models of various sizes to be successful at a top level, then models would have options when it comes to what size they can be to attain that success.

Of course, not all underweight women or models are anorexic. It is important to realize that there are, of course, models who are naturally that thin. What is unhealthy is that only very thin images are being used as an ideal for all women. It can be extremely damaging to girls' self-image—and health—to glamorize a body that the vast majority of girls would never be able to attain without developing an eating disorder and being extremely tall to begin with.

The fact is that girls are impressionable, and they will do what they can to emulate what they see in photos of models. A recent phenomenon across the country is the attainment of a "thigh gap." What is it? A thigh gap occurs when a woman stands with her feet or knees together, and her inner thighs do not touch. Numerous variables go into the amount of space between a person's thighs—like the width of the hips and pelvis—but teenage girls with poor self-esteem are vulnerable to developing eating disorders when exposed to such body trends. Models have thigh gaps, so teenage girls want thigh gaps. Models are sexy, so teenage girls want to be sexy. Models are skinny, so girls grow up with the ingrained desire to be ultrathin.

What power does being thin hold, such that Western society values it so highly? It was a revelation to me that in our culture, "skinny" is more than just a standard of beauty. For girls and women, being skinny is symbolic of popularity, wealth, success, happiness, and acceptance. Whether or not we actually pursue a career in modeling, being skinny gives us worth in the eyes of others. This mentality drives the subconscious belief that we are not enough as we are, and we need to alter ourselves to receive validation from those around us. (We'll discuss the "skinny" beauty ideal in more detail in Chapter 5.)

What happens when we believe we don't measure up to society's beauty ideals? As I mentioned in Chapter 1, regarding the girls I meet at my presentations, the result is self-loathing. Most girls and women, at one point or another, hate themselves or their bodies because they don't look as perfect as they imagine models are. However, the physical features of working models are impossible for the vast majority of women to achieve. For example, with my genetic bone structure, I could never physically meet the hip measurement required of "straight-size" models, which is 33 to 35 inches.

Before we go any further, let me explain some terminology so you can better understand the industry and the labels models are given.

The Reality of Model Sizing

"Straight-size" models represent almost 100 percent of the models you see. These models are broken down into just a few categories, for the most part: Image, Women, Fitness, and Classic Women.

"Image" models do really well in high-fashion markets, and they work with designer brands and in runway shows. These are the skinniest of all models and must be at least five nine, with a hip measurement of 33 inches, putting them at size 00 or 0.

"Women" are straight-size models who do commercial fashion work: what you see in catalogs, for brands at the mall, and on store websites. These models are between five nine and six feet, have hips that measure 33 to 35 inches, and weigh 100 to 130 pounds. These measurements put them at size 0 to 4. Even size 4 models are told on a regular basis that they need to get their measurements down. "Fitness" models have the same requirements as models in the Women division, with the exception that they can have more muscle tone. "Classic Women" is code for "old." The funny thing is that you can get put in this division at a modeling agency when you are in your 20s! The Classic Women division includes a wide range of ages, and the women who are much older than their 30s are allowed to be closer to size 6.

One reason that models are expected to be a certain size is that they need to fit in the clothing at a photo shoot. These clothes are "sample sizes" that come directly from the factory for the photo shoot months before the item will be available for purchase in stores. If a model is very small, it guarantees that the samples can be altered if needed at the shoot and still fit, versus a larger model who may not be able to get into them. So you can see the severe limitations placed on the measurements of a working model in the straight-size divisions. These expectations, by the way, create a lot of anxiety and self-loathing for models. Their bodies are continuously being monitored, and they are familiar with the pressure to be small and have experienced the judgment that comes with any deviation from the category's stringent expectations.

Last but not least is the "plus-size" or "curve" category. "Plus" models are five nine to six feet and range in size from 8 to 18. Being size 8 or 10 can be challenging, because you will appear thin on camera. Smaller plus-size models get booked mostly for swimwear and lingerie jobs. Size 12 or 14 is considered the ideal in the plus division simply because most companies' plus-size clothing samples come in size 14. When the model is size 12 or 14, the clothing samples are guaranteed to fit with only minor adjustments if the samples are on the larger side. Models who are size 16 or 18 have a hard time booking work. I know that seems crazy, since most people would consider 16 and 18 to be at the low end of "plus" sizes in the "real" world.

The Fantasy of Perfection

And now for a reality check: The average woman in the United States is five four and size 14. That's right, and that very same average woman is marketed to using images of models who are five nine and size 0 or 2. The fashion industry justifies the size disparity between models and real women by saying that models aren't meant to be real but rather aspirational. Using this approach, marketers create a feeling of strong desire or longing in potential customers. They want consumers to buy the advertised clothing because they aspire to look like the digitally altered images of unattainable bodies.

The plus-size market does the same thing, just on a different scale. After years of working as a plus-size model and talking to all kinds of plus-size women, the number one thing I hear is, "You are not plus size!" That is true! In the real world, I am not plus size. I can go into any store and buy clothing that will fit me. But in the modeling and fashion world, and in comparison to my straight-size counterparts, I am plus-size. Selling an image of a five nine, size 0 or 2 model to a woman who is five four and size 14 is as unrealistic as selling an image of a five nine, size 12 or 14 model to a woman who is five four and size 22 or 24.

Did you know that at 30 years old, I model for junior brands? When I imagine my 15-year-old self seeing modeling photos of my 30-year-old self, I realize that my 30-year-old self would be unattainable to my 15-year-old self. I looked completely different at 15 than I did at 18, and then at 25, and now at 30. In other words, the models that teenage girls are looking up to are not teenagers! For example, models for the brand aerie, which targets teenage girls, have to be at least 21 years old, according to company policy. Conversely, adolescent girls model clothes that are marketed to women! Well, that is just distorted, isn't it? Talk about unattainable!

At 15, I was still growing into myself. I believe that if I had been able to see girls who had bodies that were more representative of my teenage body, and those images were promoted and celebrated, I would have started to see myself differently. At the time, seeing models who looked like teenagers themselves would have eased the discomfort I felt as I was developing into a woman.

We have seen that girls and women who dream of looking like the models in slick, computer-enhanced advertisements or on high-fashion runways are destined to fall short. We have to remember that the images marketed to us, whether in ads or on the runway, present a fantasy of perfection that is simply not realistic. The flawless beauty attributed to models isn't attainable—even by the models themselves.

"Picture Perfect"

Unless they explicitly say otherwise, all the photos you see in magazines, on billboards, and hanging in the mall have been altered. Every single one!

Anything you can think of as far as altering a body can be done and *is* done every day using photo-editing software. Although we often hear of pictures looking "airbrushed," airbrushing was a more time-consuming, more expensive, and less effective method of alteration than the digital photo editing that is used today. In the hands of a skilled photo editor, programs such as Photoshop are capable of making alterations that are nearly impossible to see with the naked eye. You can improve the appearance of skin and remove blemishes. You can make eyes larger, breasts larger, waists smaller, hips smaller, bums smaller or bigger, thighs smaller, lips bigger, teeth whiter, and legs longer. There, I have just created an image that matches the beauty ideal! To make things worse, there are now countless apps for your phone that do the same thing in seconds. That is why it is important to stop comparing yourself with images of others; you just can't tell what is real and what is manipulated.

Victoria's Secret runway model Cameron Russell gave a controversial TED Talk in 2012 about the modeling industry, in which she compared her own photos of herself with her modeling photos. Russell told a CNN reporter: "I wanted little girls to see that models don't look like that in real life." She referred to her modeling photos as "constructions" of herself. A construction is something that is built or formed—it does not occur naturally. In other words, the images of models have been engineered to create the illusion of perfection.

There is a misconception in the general public, by the way, that models decide how photos look. I have even had girls comment on campaign images I post to my social media, asking, "Why are you so Photoshopped? I thought you were about being natural?" It is important to understand that models are never part of the creative process (hair, makeup, styling) or the editing process. Nor do they have any say in how their images are altered or retouched before being released to the public.

There is so much more to the process of creating the "perfect" photos you see than you can imagine. For example, did you know that the clothes themselves are heavily manipulated to look their ideal best?

The "Perfect" Fit

Many times I have modeled an outfit and thought, *I wouldn't be caught dead in this.* I can remember so many times shooting in an outfit that was cheaply made, ill fitting, and all around a hot mess until the stylist worked her magic.

Many people think that stylists just find amazing clothes for the stars to wear, and some do. But most stylists work on photo shoots. In that role, their job at times is to take cheaply made or ill-fitting garments and make them appear completely perfect. Stylists always have a fanny pack or purse loaded with safety pins and little industrial-strength clamps, the purpose of which is to restructure the garment from behind so that the front looks perfect. So a garment you see from the front in a photo might have loads of pins and clamps holding it and giving it shape down the back.

There are other tricks, too. For example, when we model bras and the band is too large, we often put a roll of toilet paper or paper towels between our backs and the back strap of the bra. The purpose is to pull the cups tight against our skin, giving the bra an entirely different fit and look. We also use "chicken cutlets"—fake boob inserts. Sometimes I have so many in my bra or swimsuit top that you could punch me in the chest and I wouldn't feel a thing! Yet my breasts look perfect in the clothing, making others compare their bodies negatively with mine—when the image isn't real!

The majority of plus-size clients provide size 14 or sometimes size 16 samples to shoot. Because samples vary in size depending on the client and manufacturer, and plus-size models come in various shapes and sizes, we have to bring padding to jobs. Padding can help fill out a large sample after pinning by the stylist, to ensure its shape and structure stay intact.

What exactly is the padding? Similar to football pads, model padding is the same foam as that used for dress forms in sewing. It takes the form of oval cutouts that have slim, smooth edges. It can be placed on the hips, tummy, bum, and outer thighs. Big padded bras assist in making you appear fuller on camera.

Not Measuring Up

It is important to understand these tricks of the trade because the false images they create form part of the unattainable beauty ideal and contribute to your self-esteem meltdowns! Let me break it down for you in another all-too-common scenario. You go shopping online. You see a dress that you like on a model who is five ten and size 0 or 2. What you are seeing in the photo is not a true depiction of how that dress actually fits, because it has been altered to conform to the model's body perfectly, just for the photo. The model has had the benefit of an hour and a half of professional hair and makeup, plus great lighting on set. The selected image has then been sent to the photo editor, who perfectly retouches the model's skin and body shape as well as any part of the dress that did not photograph well. That image gets loaded on to the website—and into your subconscious mind when you make your purchase.

I love that dress, you think as you excitedly order it and wait for it to arrive. You get a rush as you open your package and see that beautiful dress for the first time. You have to try it on right away and then . . . it happens. Your excitement and happiness turn to disappointment and sadness as you look in the mirror: the dress looks nothing like the image stored in your mind of "how that dress should look"! You then think negative thoughts about your body—as though it had some evil plot to humiliate you—when, in reality, that dress *never looked like it did in the photo.*

There have been many times that I have actually felt guilty because the clothes I modeled were terrible, but the stylist and I made them look amazing. I knew women or girls were going to buy the clothing because the picture looked so good, but what they were actually getting was nowhere near as cute as the image portrayed. And yet this is the very reason models exist. A model's real job is not to represent beauty, be inspiring, or be a role model for young girls. The job of a model is to *sell products.*

How Attainable Is the Goal of Modeling?

A number of girls do become models. They are genetically predisposed to the job, and they possibly sacrifice their health for it. But just how achievable is the goal of becoming a working model—especially the kind that young girls tend to aspire to, the kind that gets lots of attention?

I used to want to be a Victoria's Secret model. Well, hasn't every girl thought about how amazing that would be? If you are a model and get selected to be one of the "Angels" for the Victoria's Secret Fashion Show, the show makes you instantly famous and shoots your career to the top. Who wouldn't want that? There it is again . . . that desire to be beautiful, happy, successful, empowered, and loved.

While doing research for my Re-Model Me workshops, I came across a video of Ed Razek, the current president and chief marketing officer of Limited Brands, the parent company of Victoria's Secret. Commenting on the casting for the upcoming 2012 Victoria's Secret Fashion Show, he said, "Having this runway show in your résumé is a very big thing because out of six billion people, less than thirty get to do it! That's one in one hundred million women." (Note that the show has apparently gotten bigger over time, featuring around 50 models in 2015.) Here comes some logic to put things into perspective.

One in 100 million odds sound crazy, but just how crazy are they? The BBC reports the odds of being killed by lightning in your lifetime as 1 in 300,000. Yikes! Consider the odds of a high school basketball star becoming a professional athlete; the National Collegiate Athletic Association (NCAA) estimates that the odds for men are 1 in 3,333 and for women are 1 in 4,000. A young woman is 25,000 times more likely to become a pro athlete than a model in the Victoria's Secret Fashion Show.

We want to be in the Victoria's Secret Fashion Show for the fame, money, success, and lifestyle that come with it—or so we are led to believe. So some of us put our bodies through hell in hopes of having the chance to "make it," while others put our hearts and minds through hell by obsessing about it. Interestingly enough, we have much better odds of becoming a *billionaire*, with a 1 in 7 million chance! Which makes me think, if we can become independently wealthy on our own and create our own success, why are we wasting so much time trying or wishing to be what one company has deemed "beautiful"?

Some of you may now be thinking about the many other women who are living their dreams, even when others told them it was not possible. What about women who have made tremendous achievements in life, also by overcoming great odds, whom society admires? I'm talking about achievements as diverse as winning an Olympic gold medal, becoming a rock star, traveling in space, having a script made into a Hollywood movie, and creating a successful brand. You may be thinking, *If they can achieve their dreams, then why can't I?*

It *is* possible that a future Victoria's Secret model is reading this right now. There are girls out there who have the right DNA and fit what that brand is looking for. However, it is important to understand that the inspiring feats I listed above are arrived at through intelligence, hard work, practice, skill, determination, and confidence in your abilities. Modeling, on the other hand, is based on your appearance first and foremost. I didn't do anything special to have my face and body; it is my DNA. If you don't fit the requirements set by the industry, you immediately fail. No amount of effort, research, schooling, talent, or belief in yourself will help you overcome the odds against becoming a model if your face and body don't look how others say they should. In that case, pursuing modeling as your dream would be damaging to your mental and physical well-being.

Jeopardizing Your Health for an Ideal

Before you think, "I want to be a model so badly that I'll brave the astronomical odds against it," I want to share with you another aspect of what it takes to be a model—specifically, the questionable training regimen required prior to the fashion show. Melissa Whitworth from *The Telegraph* of London sat down with Adriana Lima in 2011 to get the real scoop on what it takes to be a Victoria's Secret model. Models always tell the public, "I eat whatever I want." But people in the industry know this is not true. Lima revealed her real diet leading up to walking the Victoria's Secret runway show, and I'm sure I wasn't the only one who found it quite shocking.

The article states, "She sees a nutritionist, who has measured her body's muscle mass, fat ratio and levels of water retention. He prescribes protein shakes, vitamins and supplements to keep Lima's energy levels up during this training period. Lima drinks a gallon of water a day. For nine days before the show, she will drink only protein shakes—'no solids.' The concoctions include powdered egg. Two days before the show, she will abstain from the daily gallon of water, and 'just drink normally.' Then, 12 hours before the show, she will stop drinking entirely." All this is done while also working out with her trainer twice a day. "No liquids at all so you dry out, sometimes you can lose up to eight pounds just from that," Lima told *The Telegraph*.

When you work as a model, you know what girls are doing to their bodies to maintain the industry's extreme size requirements. A diet like this would be viewed as normal. Therefore, I believe Lima disclosed this information without realizing that the general public would find it shocking and extreme, if not unhealthy. Despite some negative attention, Victoria's Secret continues to use underweight models. The idea that treating your body in an unhealthy way is acceptable because you are rewarded for your actions is why we have a culture of so many sick girls and women who do not value their bodies or their health.

The truth is that we do not need to be models to be beautiful, happy, successful, empowered, and loved. All girls and women (including models) have an opportunity to discover what beauty means to them individually, outside what they have been taught to believe. Like health, beauty is not one-dimensional; it is limitless, and as soon as we begin to understand that, we will no longer see ourselves through our insecurities. Instead, we will perceive the beauty of our mind, body, and spirit.

What brands like Victoria's Secret have been so successful in doing is creating the "want" in us. We do not *need* to be a model, but we have been made to believe we should *want* to be one—and should do our best to make this desire a reality—despite the fact that the goal is virtually unattainable, not to mention unhealthy, and we have much better odds of being struck by lightning or becoming a billionaire.

■ ■ ■

When it comes to the dream of becoming a model or at least looking like one, it is clear that the reality is far darker than the image portrayed. We can't accept the claim of advertisers that their expertly styled and edited images of models are aspirational—that they are not intended to represent reality. Hopefully, now that you know about the manipulations going on behind the scenes to create the images you see in the media every day, you will be less tempted to compare yourself to an unattainable beauty ideal. In Chapter 3, we further examine the harm caused by believing in and pursuing this unattainable ideal.

■ ■ ■ ■ ■

Chapter 3

How the Beauty Ideal Brings Us Down

Although advertisers claim that models and the photos they use of them to sell their products are meant to be aspirational rather than reflections of reality, there is a part of us that just doesn't seem to get that. We can hear it, yet for some reason, we're reluctant to let it really sink in.

The fact is, the media has painted the perfect picture of how our lives should look, beginning with our favorite movies from childhood that were played on a loop and progressing over time into our favorite romantic comedies and TV shows. These stories and ideas create expectations and desires that can be far from realistic. The message sent to girls and women by the media is that in order for us to be successful in achieving our fairytale ending and finally feeling the love we have been searching for, we need a Prince Charming to come riding into the picture on his white horse. According to the majority of health and fashion magazines, you will get your Prince Charming when you get hot! Then and only then will you be worthy of the love story you have been waiting to experience.

The Media's Reinforcement of the Beauty Ideal

Ali, a friend of mine who is a preschool teacher, shared with me an interesting experience she had at work. She asked a few kids who were standing by her, "What is beauty?" A little boy said, "Princesses are beauty!" It's clear that both women and men are programmed with the beauty ideal from a young age. It is not only a specific image of beauty we have been trained to desire but also what the attainment of that image symbolizes in our society.

Beauty ideals have been used to sell products to women and also to sell cultural beliefs about women's value. For instance, advertisements in the early 20th century would often tell women that if they were more beautiful, then they would have a better chance at being chosen as a wife. Being married was a societal expectation of women, and being a good housewife—which included being physically pleasing to your man—was an integral part of a woman's value. Has your mother or grandmother ever mentioned your weight or hair in relevance to finding a husband? My grandmother has—many times.

Many advertisements from the 1950s reinforce the programming my grandmother received. One ad I remember in particular featured a skinny woman and a curvy woman in swimsuits standing next to each other. The writing across the top of the ad said, "How do you look in your bathing suit? Skinny? Thousands gain 10 to 25 pounds this quick easy way!" (Back then the beauty ideal was a full hourglass figure rather than today's ultraskinny ideal.)

If we step back and look objectively at our culture's beliefs about beauty, we can see an expectation that women's bodies are meant to be pleasing to others, not to themselves. When we buy into the belief that beauty is external and that it is what matters about women most, then that which lies *inside* us isn't valued. It simply doesn't count.

How the Beauty Ideal Shortchanges Us All

The media's narrow definition of beauty excludes the vast majority of women from being viewed as attractive. By selling people an image of what a perfect life should look like instead of allowing people to discover what kind of life is perfect for them, we all miss out on the opportunity to enjoy the beauty all around us in its various shapes and forms. It also leads us into unhealthy partnerships and friendships that are based on our insecurities and on using each other for what we think the other gives us. Relationships like these look good only on the surface and ultimately rob us of the opportunity for healthy relationships—those meaningful, truly loving connections that make us happy and our lives feel worthwhile.

Human beings naturally want companions in life, and when you find a person who loves and respects you, it can be the best bond on earth. I think we women need to take a look at what exactly we are being trained to want when it comes to a partner. Do we want to meet a person we love, respect, enjoy, and connect with on a deeper level? Or does our desire for romantic attention stem from a fear of being unlovable and alone? If subconsciously we believe that only if we have attention are we then of value, then we are harming our self-esteem as well as our chances for a meaningful and enduring love.

Understanding Your Self-Esteem Meltdowns

Bombarded by the unending barrage of unrealistic images, we constantly compare ourselves—totally negatively, of course—with the bodies we see in them. Tossing out logic, we look without question at what our society tells us is beautiful, and feel self-loathing wash over us in that moment of inadequacy as we tell ourselves how miserably we fall short. Rather than saying, "Real life isn't like that. I'm beautiful the way I am," we say, "That's how I should be. What a failure and loser I am! I need to fix myself!"

To make matters worse, we rarely step out of this pattern of thinking and feeling long enough to even glimpse a new perspective. Our brains have simply become accustomed to these images, no matter how unrealistic they are, because in our culture they are now the norm for advertising fashion, beauty, and other kinds of products. The result is a continual erosion of our self-esteem.

What happens, for example, when we see young girls posing sexily in ad campaigns? Let's say we recognize the model and happen to know that she's 16, even though she looks more mature in the ad. Do we logically compare that image with what we know to be true about what life is really like at 16 or do we just buy into it wholesale? In my experience, at that age girls are excited to get their driver's license and get their braces off, and are worried about passing the next math test. Maybe they even have their first boyfriend, or are excited to go to the school dance. I don't know about you, but when I was 16 I was uncomfortable with my body and was not like the "sexpot" image of young girls we see all over the media today.

Despite this, my guess is that when you see those types of images, you don't even think about your own experience at 16, or your family members who are currently that age, or other 16-year-old girls you see in real life. Instead, you probably compare the image with yourself at your *current* age, whatever that happens to be, and may even have a few thoughts like, *Wow, I wish my body looked like that,* which could lead to, *I feel gross, and I need to work out,* and then, *Maybe I will try those jeans she has on. They might make my butt look better.* The exact same things happen with the plus-size markets, by the way, only with the curvier bodies of size 8 to 18 models creating the aspirational effect on the unsuspecting consumer. The result is the same: "That looks so good on her; maybe I should buy it." (Of course, we don't see any of the Photoshop used or the pins, clips, and padding necessary to make the clothes fit the model in a way they never could in reality.)

Let's continue with our scenario. What typically happens when you get lured into buying some clothing through the subconscious desire to look like the model who was wearing it? You guessed it: *self-esteem meltdown.* Yep, I'm talking tears in the dressing room. We've all been there. Nothing fits! Maybe you've already ripped the seams on one shirt and couldn't get the shorts you grabbed up over your butt. It's hot, and you just feel fat and disgusting. Or perhaps you're really thin and everything you put on is baggy and shapeless, and you're wishing you had more curves in the right places. Whatever the situation, we share the same tears, frustration, and meltdowns, only for seemingly different reasons. However, it *is* ultimately for the same reason: we are all trying to live up to the beauty ideal. And we respond the same way:

pointing the finger at ourselves for not being the way we "should" be rather than seeing that we've bought into an unattainable ideal that has made us blind to our own beauty exactly as we are.

Falseness in the "Real" Campaigns

In an ironic parallel, as much as our minds are overloaded with messages about the limited and narrow definition of beauty by companies that wish to sell us products based on our insecurities, we are also seeing an increase in "body-positive" messaging from advertisers in the attempt to sell to us based on our desire to feel enough just as we are. Such campaigns include Dove's "Real Beauty" and aerie's "aerie Real." To me, these campaigns' use of the word *real* indicates that they are aware of the unrealistic and harmful imaging of typical advertising and implies that their images are a more truthful reflection of what women really look like. But is this truly the case?

The one thing you must remember is that corporations and advertisers all share the same agenda—to sell products and make money. No pun intended, but that is the bottom line! With that in mind, let's look more closely at one of these examples—the "aerie Real" campaign. In spring 2014, American Eagle Outfitters's sister brand for intimates and swimwear, aerie, launched a campaign called "aerie Real." Its ads featured *unretouched* photos of models in bras, underwear, and apparel. The aerie brand targets 15- to 21-year-olds—so the campaign reaches young women at a time when their body confidence is so often influenced by the media. While I love the campaign's concept, when I look at the brand, I immediately see inconsistencies in the messaging and the imagery used to promote it.

For example, every single girl featured on the aerie brand website is a professional model, and the vast majority are in the straight-size category. (As a reminder, that means a size 4 or under, while being five nine or taller.) None of the product pages for the aerie brand reflects a "real" diverse mix of body types or beauty for teenage girls. Rather, the aerie brand image reflects the same beauty ideal other companies are promoting to sell products to teenage girls, and in some cases the same models are used for these competing brands.

Having worked as a plus-size model for my entire career, I've noticed how common it is for a photo shoot to feature just one model who is larger than the other models. We are the token "big friend" in the group shot of straight-size models. When I look at the campaign images for aerie, I notice the same thing; there is just the one larger model in each group. But if we're keeping things real here, shouldn't the size distribution in the group be reversed? Out of a group of five girls, wouldn't it be more realistic to show just one straight-size model, since those proportions are so rare? Then the other models could be chosen who fit the range of sizes that aerie offers, from medium to curvy. Wouldn't this mix reflect a more realistic group of friends?

That being said, aerie is doing a great job featuring all types of "real girls" and more realistic bodies on social media. It is important to understand that most companies are simply following their old formulas for success based on a society conditioned to consume aspirational ideals. When a company deviates from the tried-and-tested, they want evidence to show that their new idea (such as using relatable rather than aspirational models) would have the same selling power, so they're not risking millions of dollars for no reason. It's easy to look at a brand and say all the things they *should* be doing but much harder to make it happen in real life. So while I'd love to see more reality in the "real" campaigns, the approaches currently taken can be a way for a company to test the waters before fully committing.

One aspect of "real" beauty campaigns that companies use to try to appear different from competitors is the *idea* that these models are "real"—but, then again, what makes something real enough? Dove's "Real Beauty" campaigns are well known for featuring a variety of women, especially in an older demographic. While they sell an image of average, everyday women, their casting criteria reads: no tattoos, no scars, flawless skin, beautiful hair, and bodies that fall nicely between "not too curvy" and "not too athletic." Clearly this eliminates a large percentage of women.

Still, when I first learned of Dove's campaign, it seemed like a wonderful message and opportunity, so I asked my agent to look into working with them. He had to inform me that although I seemed to fit Dove's criteria on paper, I was not eligible to model for them because I was "too pretty"; this, apparently, makes me not real enough.

Be pretty, but not *too* pretty, don't be too skinny or curvy or athletic—we seem to have very narrow standards for "real" in the media. While a brand might tout the message, "We are all beautiful, and 'real' should be celebrated," it also says, "Real women and girls look like *this*; this is who should be confident and love their flaws." Most brands aren't quite the all-inclusive definition of real beauty that they make themselves out to be, but these could be powerful steps in the right direction. As consumers, we must keep pushing brands to portray more diversity and celebrate all women. When we understand that both the aspirational image of beauty and "real" beauty are manipulated and geared toward selling products, it allows us the opportunity to disconnect from those labels altogether.

We can *all* be aspirational, and we are all 100 percent real no matter what we look like.

The Message of Not Being Enough

I understand that the "real" marketing concept is one that girls will respond positively to, at least at first. Girls are searching for something they can see themselves in that will reflect who they are. Because they have such low self-esteem, the hope that these "real" campaigns gives them will initially create a happy feeling. They will have a positive emotional reaction to the campaign because it connects to their desire to be accepted as they are. Because of this, girls will also have a positive brand association and want to buy the products. But what happens once the products are used and these young girls realize they do not look like the models in the unretouched images? What happens when they begin to ask, "Why do the girls in the aerie pictures look so much prettier than me, and they are not even retouched?" Or, "Why doesn't my stomach look like that?" Or, "Why do all the Dove women have perfect skin?" Or, "Why doesn't my body look like that?" This type of "real" campaign might ultimately land a more serious blow to girls' self-esteem.

Don't get me wrong. The idea that more brands are not altering photos of models and opting to leave in a little scar or stretch mark is, in my opinion, a step in the right direction. My intention here is not to pick apart this or similar brands or campaigns, because I would like to see more companies question and expand their currently limited definitions of beauty. But it is important to be aware that, no matter what, corporations want your money and are always selling you something. We must always look beneath the surface to see what message is *really* being conveyed, or else it will get filed into our subconscious and potentially influence us negatively without our knowing it. (This is a topic we will soon look much more closely at.)

Some Ramifications of Buying Into the Beauty Ideal

So what *are* some of the ways we are harmed by the unattainable beauty ideal and the steady stream of images and messaging fed to us by the media and advertisers promoting it as something that we should aspire to achieve? Below are but a few stories from my personal experience, illustrating how this can impact us. The first group of examples shows how buying into the beauty ideal can cause us to deny ourselves some of life's (small or large) joys.

Kaelan

I started working with Kaelan, a model with Natural Model Management (NMM), when she was 18 years old and fresh out of high school. We were shooting an agency promotion at the beach and asked Kaelan to be part of it. We shot images of our models in various swimwear, and then we sent those images to current and potential clients. Kaelan did amazingly and looked adorable in her red monokini.

Since she lived only a few miles from the beach, we offered to give Kaelan a ride home after the photo shoot. While in the car, she thanked my husband, Bradford, and me for such a great day. She said, "I have never worn my swimsuit around other girls and felt comfortable. This is the first time that I could see other girls with bodies similar to mine enjoying themselves at the beach and not covering up. All my friends are so small and petite; I have always felt so fat.

But today I was able to see that all the different bodies were beautiful in their natural form, and it was really nice not having to suck in all day."

As Kaelan's story shows, when we don't look the way we are told we should look and we negatively compare ourselves with others or the images we see, we often deny ourselves wonderful experiences, like enjoying a day at the beach. This denial of joy takes on other forms as well.

Joan

I was stuck at the Denver airport waiting for my delayed flight back home to Palm Springs. My phone was about to die, so I walked over to the nearest plug to charge it. A woman there warned me that the socket I was attempting to use was broken, and she was kind enough to allow me to use the extra USB outlet in her plugged-in charger. When I plugged my USB cord into her plug, the weight made her charger fall out of the wall! After an awkward laugh, I went straight into problem-solving mode, using my laptop's weight to wedge her charger in the wall. We high-fived, and that was the beginning of a great conversation with one inspiring woman.

Joan was a 67-year-old professional golfer, headed to Palm Springs for a tournament. She'd been a top-level tennis player when she was younger, despite the fact that Title IX had not yet given girls equal access to sports in schools or opportunities to play in college. She said she hadn't cared; she'd loved it and was good at it, plus she'd never been a "girlie-girl." She told me that she hadn't even picked up a golf club until she was 39 years old! I thought that was incredible. She gave me a pep talk about how I am capable of anything I put my mind to, and I believed her.

She then asked me what I do. When people ask me that question, I never know exactly what I am going to say; it just depends on the person. In her case, I knew she would appreciate all the things we do with Healthy Is the New Skinny, and I was right. She loved everything about it. She then shared with me how she had recently lost 80 pounds doing the paleo diet. At this point our flight was boarding, so we were walking and talking. Joan was fast becoming my idol, but then I heard her say, "Yeah, I've lost eighty pounds and I just want to lose ten more, but my body won't budge. I work out and stay on my diet, but I can't seem to lose those last ten pounds."

She added, "Pizza is my favorite thing in the world, and I haven't had a slice in two years!" In my mind I was saying, *Nooooo! The most badass, cool, inspiring lady I have ever met hasn't had a piece of pizza in two years. Nooooooo!* The idea of needing to lose those last 10 pounds had robbed Joan of something she truly enjoys. She was made to believe that she must deny herself in order to be good enough according to some societal ideal.

Natalie

The damage doesn't stop there. An unattainable beauty ideal can easily lead to self-loathing, shame, and a sense of failure. Take Natalie, for example. At five nine and around 165 pounds, she is tall and what the general public would view as at a healthy weight, if not thin. She is 42 and a successful writer and editor who is dedicated to working on projects that make a positive difference in the world. She also revealed to me that she keeps photos of Victoria's Secret models in her desk drawer. Why? As a reminder of the ideal she wants to be.

So what happens when Natalie looks at those photos? She feels a sense of failure—of not being good enough—because, as a dancer in her youth, she used to have a body that was 135 pounds with very little body fat. Even though she had not danced regularly in many, many years and spends most of her day sitting at her computer for work, she wants to look the same as she did in her teens and early 20s. Unfortunately, Natalie's own perfectionistic tendencies have been compounded by the expectations of the man in her life, who has always been attracted to the "model-thin" look. These things have made her self-critical and feel inadequate when looking at Victoria's Secret models. Despite being successful in her career and steeped in passion and purpose, Natalie still keeps the images close as a reminder of what she is striving for—creating a continual feeling of just not quite being good enough unless she achieves it.

Suzie

Natalie isn't the only one who has used Victoria's Secret models as "thinspiration." Many girls and women do it, and sometimes the shame and self-loathing can lead to really hurting ourselves. Suzie, one of the models we represent at NMM, for example, struggled for years with the belief that she needed to be like "them" in order to be beautiful. Suzie grew up in a wealthy community where there is a lot of pressure to look "perfect." She is an all-American, beautiful blonde with a tall, strong frame.

When Suzie was a freshman in high school, the only thing she felt was stopping her from achieving her dream of being the "popular hot girl" was her weight. Suzie was not overweight by any means, but she interpreted her size 12 body on a five-eleven frame as "fat." When I asked her why she thought that, she replied, "Because no one ever told me there were different body types. I thought there were just different levels of fat and I was at the high end and needed to lose weight so I could be with the other girls on the low end of the fat scale."

When Suzie first came to this conclusion about herself, she covered her walls in images of runway and Victoria's Secret models as a reminder of her newfound goals. Suzie then started on the Atkins Diet and cut out all carbs. She lost 30 pounds and immediately began getting the attention she was seeking to validate her acceptableness. When the weight loss plateaued, Suzie took extreme measures—developing a horrible eating disorder, and even secretly turning to drugs—in hopes of forcing her body past the breaking point. Her negative life cycle consumed her identity and the choices she made for herself, all because of an unattainable image of beauty she had accepted as a truth.

Katie

I was once there myself. When I was 18, I went to New York City to model and attend art school. I had never lived on my own or had to care for myself 100 percent. There was a Chinese food take-out place next to my dorm that was so good and cheap. There was also pizza down the street and delis on every block. Not to mention that cooking was not something I knew how to do, nor could I afford the grocery bill at any NYC grocery stores.

My mom had been a single parent the majority of my life, and I was raised on fast food. Eating an unhealthy diet was something I was used to. I only realize now that the reason I always felt terrible and had zero energy while playing sports was because my body was malnourished. When I got to NYC, my eating habits didn't really change. What did change, however, was that I stopped playing competitive sports. When you take what I was eating and subtract the two to three hours of daily physical activity, you are left with the "freshman 15," only in my case I gained 25 pounds.

I was definitely in denial about it. I would buy clothes and think to myself, *Why are they sizing all of their clothes wrong? I am a size 12, not 14!* Then I did the subconscious sorting of my clothes, and all the tight-fitting jeans got shoved back where I wouldn't notice them. There was a sudden increase in stretchy material followed by a total freak-out one day when I decided to face reality and step on the scale. *Two hundred pounds?!? WTF?!?* was my first thought . . . just being honest. I felt shock, then sadness, shame, humiliation, anger . . . and then fear. *How did this happen? How am I going to fix it? What is everyone saying about me? Am I always going to be fat?*

I remember walking home from art school that day. It was December, and students at my dorm were beginning to go home for the holidays, including my roommate, so the dorm was pretty empty. There I was, depressed, alone, and feeling really pathetic to have let myself get so "fat." So I decided that I would search for a solution. While I was at a drugstore, I just happened to notice the diet pill aisle. What a coincidence finding myself there! I grabbed a bottle of pills and headed back to my dorm room to study up on them. The warning label said the pills could cause sporadic heartbeats . . . blah blah blah . . . and if a pill gets lodged in your throat, you could *die!* It still alarms me to this day that I didn't care about the warnings of possible heart attack and instead was focused on the size of these pills—because they were huge! I have never been good at taking pills, and I thought for sure one was going to get stuck in my throat.

So there I was, sitting alone in my dorm room with nothing but my giant diet pills, hoping for a miracle. In that moment it was my dissatisfaction with myself, along with my shame, guilt, and fear, controlling my decision making. I wanted so badly to be "fixed," I didn't care what the consequences of my actions were. I gave it a shot, and the first pill went down, but not without some gagging and eye watering. I pumped myself up for the second round and put the pill in my mouth, followed by a huge gulp of water. The massive pill turned sideways and, yep, got stuck in my throat! I immediately drank more water to try to force it down, but that didn't work. It hurt to swallow, and it wasn't budging. I ran down the hall to the kitchen and grabbed some crackers and started to shove those in my mouth. At this point I was really scared; I was eating and drinking, hoping to knock the pill loose.

I remember coming back into my dorm room and lying on the floor. I just lay there, looking at the ceiling and thinking, *I am going to die from a diet pill and no one will find me until after Christmas break.* Not to mention the news reports: "Plus-size model dies alone in dorm room. The cause of her death remains unclear, but her body was covered in crackers and a bottle of diet pills was found by her side." Yes, I can say this was an all-time low point.

Well, the pill eventually went down. I didn't die, so that was great, but I did feel completely uncomfortable with myself on all levels. I never took a diet pill after that experience. I did, however, try every diet known to man. I tried Atkins, and just ended up being miserable and really constipated. I tried the South Beach Diet, but it required a lot of cooking, which wasn't realistic for me. I got a trainer at the gym and was walking two and a half miles each way to and from the gym on top of my hour-long session with my trainer. I did spin class. Aerobics. I even signed up for a weight-loss program where you go to an office and get weighed two times per week. I could eat only their bars, snacks, and drinks, and then I had to make my meals. I lost seven pounds the first week because they had me drink a gallon of this juice-type stuff instead of eating. So basically I didn't lose pounds of fat; I just wasn't eating, and as soon as I started eating again, I gained the seven pounds back. I had spent so much time, energy, and money on diets trying to lose weight and couldn't figure out why nothing seemed to work!

Know that all the effort I was putting into losing weight had nothing to do with the goal of good health. I had no education on health whatsoever. I had no clue what being healthy meant, let alone what it looked like or how it felt. I was merely equating working out and dieting with having the "ideal body." I thought "health" was an image and something I could buy, and I tried—with no good results. The same way I didn't care if taking a diet pill would damage my heart, I didn't even think about how being active could reduce my chance of heart disease, which is the number one killer of women in the United States. I couldn't have cared less if I was gaining muscle and losing fat; if the number on the scale didn't go down, I thought I was failing. All I knew was that if I could just lose weight, that would render me worthy of love in our society.

I realize now that good health is not something I can buy; it is something that I and every other person must develop and achieve over time with intention, attention, and care. Just like Suzie, Joan, Natalie, and Kaelan, I was punishing myself for not being how others told me I should be in order to be acceptable and worthy of love. I was secretly beating myself up inside and operating on negative thinking and emotions while expecting a positive result. I would deny myself joy and happiness because, in my mind, I only deserved those things if I was skinny—if I lost "those last 10 pounds."

We need to recognize the potential harm we can cause our bodies by undereating and overexercising in the attempt to be skinny. By starving our bodies of food and nutrients, we increase our odds of heart failure due to a slowing heart rate and low blood pressure. We are more likely to develop osteoporosis, which means our bone density will begin to weaken and our bones may become brittle and easier to break. That's not all; we can experience muscle loss and dehydration, which can lead to kidney failure. We may not be able to see these warning signs, but that doesn't mean they can't be fatal. Our bodies deserve better than this.

What Else Those Last 10 Pounds Cost Us

I was just on Instagram yesterday and read a comment from a woman in her mid-20s who I feel is a great example to use here. She liked the sweatpants we were selling in the posted photo. She commented to a friend, "I love these. Maybe if I lose those five pounds I will get them as a reward." When I looked at her photo, I could see that she was not overweight. Why would she be able to enjoy sweatpants she liked only if she lost five pounds? Why would you get a reward for losing five pounds?

The need to lose 5 to 10 more pounds is something I have heard from girls and women of all ages. "If I can just lose those last five to ten pounds . . ." Then, what? You can be happy? Worthy of all good things? I'd like for you to really think about this for a minute—about how harsh and unloving this mind-set really is!

What's clear from these examples is that being fixated on our bodies causes us to hold back from living to our full potential. I found it quite sad when I finally realized that, by being so preoccupied with all of this, I was keeping myself small, totally distracted from creating a meaningful life out of who I truly was as a human being.

What's also clear is that I am far from the only woman to have fallen prey to the toxic messaging and social programming creating the constant sense of self-loathing that keeps us distracted and small. Way too many girls and women are raised with beliefs about ourselves that make us feel like crap. We get sucked into a "glass-half-empty" mentality and because we have been operating on self-loathing, anxiety, and the fear of being unlovable our whole lives, we don't have the tools to make a change and free ourselves. While we have a vague awareness from the pain we feel that something is wrong, we don't know what it is or what will help make it stop. So when we try to make changes and to feel better, we fail. Our failure reinforces what I call this "negative life cycle," and it magnifies and becomes all-consuming. Part of the reason I'm sharing all these stories with you is to show you that *you are not alone*. Every single woman reading this book will become aware of her own negative thinking and will then be able to reflect on the effect it has had on her life choices and the way she keeps herself feeling "less than" and thus disengaged from her *real* calling in life.

■ ■ ■

We are all guilty of this type of thinking at one point or another. To break out of it, instead of asking ourselves, "What can I do to lose weight?" we need to stop and ask ourselves, "Why do I *really* feel bad?" We need to go down the path to uncover the answers to why we feel the way we do and where our value as women and as human beings *really* comes from. (I promise you, it's not the mirror or the scale.)

In the next chapters, we go deeper into the world of the media and advertising and explore how and why it is a prime source for many of the messages we get about our world, ourselves, and our worth.

■ ■ ■ ■ ■

Chapter 4

Desire and the Subconscious: It All Started with a Man Named Freud

By this point, we are beginning to really see that the modeling, fashion, and advertising industries are built on illusion and thrive on our insecurities. The beauty ideal they've got us all trying to live up to is unattainable, and it isn't even real! It doesn't get more manipulative than that. It reminds me a lot of one of my favorite classic films, *The Wizard of Oz*. Dorothy, the Cowardly Lion, the Tin Man, and the Scarecrow brave the long journey to Emerald City to see the great and powerful Wizard of Oz in the hopes that he will give them each what they feel is missing from their lives, what will make them whole. What they come to discover, of course, is that the Wizard isn't a wizard at all, that he is nothing but an ordinary man behind a curtain who has no special power to grant wishes, and that what they were seeking was inside them the whole time.

So how is it that we are so susceptible to this kind of deception? That's what I hope to address in this chapter and the next. We cover topics like where our beauty ideal comes from—who is behind the curtain and what purpose it serves for them. We examine why advertisers and marketing firms put so much energy into perpetuating this illusion. To understand this, we must first understand something about how advertising works . . . and to understand that, we must first understand some basics about human psychology. This chapter is a brief look into certain aspects of the human mind that lay the groundwork for understanding what and why you buy.

A Beautiful Realization

To help you unlock your shackles from our culture's beauty ideal, I am going to share some eye-opening information. First, I'd like to tell you a bit about how I stumbled on this information, as I hope that reading about my discovery process will encourage you to look for solutions to what isn't working in your own life.

I was on a modeling job in Lanzarote, one of the Canary Islands off the western coast of Africa, and I was feeling frustrated and stuck. I was searching for a deeper meaning for Healthy Is the New Skinny (HNS) as a social movement, as well as a fuller understanding of my own purpose in life and how I could be of greater service to the world. Although I have always had a sense that my purpose was to lift up and empower the female spirit, at that point I still had so much to learn. I needed a big-picture understanding of the problem to really begin contributing solutions that would make a significant difference in people's lives.

I was also tired. I felt as if I had been working my butt off day in and day out, and although I was making ground with the message behind HNS, it was all-consuming. I was building my brand, my modeling agency, and my career as a model and new author, but I was unable to connect the dots as to why this was my unique journey and contribution to make. I was searching for *something* that could help me make sense of who I was and what I wanted. I wanted to understand: How do all the aspects of my life and experiences connect? What is the purpose and deeper learning from each of them?

As I began to ask more questions and examine the answers more closely, I realized that until now I'd been protected from outside negativity through the power of my genuine desire to make a difference and my naïveté. I truly believed that I could do it, and so I did. I truly believed that I could make a difference in the modeling industry. I truly believed I could help girls use modeling as a vehicle to earn a great living and to travel, and provide them with tools to encourage them not to identify with modeling as their source of value. I wanted girls to be empowered the way I had been empowered. I wanted to run a business with integrity, honesty, and kindness.

I'd started Natural Model Management and Healthy Is the New Skinny to accomplish all of that, but after four years, my views had changed. I realized some difficult truths about myself, people, business, and the world in general. I felt exhausted and overwhelmed and as though I were constantly fighting to not become like the very people who inspired me to create a different, better way to do business. (Even now, I still have days like this!) At this point, I was starting to have the same misgivings about being a business owner that I did about being a model. Even with success, I felt unfulfilled and conflicted in my heart. I realized my dream may need some adjusting—my dream of being a business owner, like my dream of being a model, did not come as advertised.

There I was, sitting in my quiet hotel room, exhausted and jet-lagged but unable to sleep. I had been chatting with a friend online about some of my frustrations and feelings of disappointment I was trying to work through. She sent me a link to a documentary and told me I had to watch it.

Once I began watching, I was hooked! I know I must have had bags under my eyes the next day at work because I stayed up almost all night watching this film. After being exposed to the information it contained, I started to see my life more clearly. What I discovered was the final piece of the puzzle and my life's purpose up to that point.

The British documentary series I watched, *The Century of the Self*, takes a deep look into human consciousness. It is the key to understanding how we are manipulated by corporations and the media, why we don't love who we are, and why our self-loathing is not an accident but an absolute necessity for a consumer society like ours to thrive and for corporations to make money. After all, who are the number one consumers in the world? Americans. Who among Americans are targeted the most to purchase products? Women. How do companies convince you to purchase products you don't need? Well, that's one of the things we're going to look at more closely coming up. It all started with Freud's revelatory discoveries about the human sense of self.

Before I explain to you the role Freud's theories played in the creation of public relations and advertising, I want you to quickly do a little exercise: Stop for a moment and think of a really beautiful woman. Just let an image of whatever you consider a really beautiful woman come to mind. What do you see? Now, very important, ask yourself: *Where* did that image come from? Does it truly reflect your own original definition of beauty? How much of it do you imagine was influenced by all the images the media has been feeding you as "beautiful" since practically the day you were born?

While every person reading this book may have a slightly different picture, my guess is that many of those images reflect the same narrow ideal. When I did this exercise, I realized that my picture of female beauty did not truly come from me. I also realized that the dreams I had of *being* a "beautiful" woman had been implanted in my mind, as well. Learning how this was accomplished enabled me to discover the truth about myself—who I am and why I am here.

Waking Up

For the longest time, I would hear people talk about "being conscious," but I wasn't really sure what that meant. I thought it meant being aware of myself and how I treated others. While I wasn't completely wrong, it wasn't until I learned about Sigmund Freud that I got a bit more understanding of the depth of the human mind and consciousness.

Freud, often called the father of psychoanalysis, developed radical new theories about human consciousness and the subconscious. By analyzing humans, their thought processes, and how they conformed to fit into society, Freud articulated the ideas that every human being has a conscious mind that is present and aware and a subconscious mind that stores information that the conscious mind is unaware of. Freud believed the subconscious mind stores hidden desires and animalistic impulses that drive our decision making and behavior.

He used the analogy of an iceberg to explain the mind's complexity. The tip of the iceberg, the part above water, is our conscious mind, which is operating in the moment and which we are aware of. Hidden below the surface is the subconscious mind, although we are not aware of its presence or its effect on our current decision making. Freud focused on human desire and how humans repress parts of themselves that are not viewed as acceptable by society. We all have emotions and thoughts that we repress, stored in the subconscious mind. We are prone to act out unconsciously on these repressed desires, and they are often the true underlying cause of a behavior.

Also stored in your subconscious is the societal and media messaging that is bombarding you. How many messages are you exposed to each day? Back in 1998, *The New York Times* reported, "Studies show that the typical consumer is bombarded by 5,000 advertising messages a day." And that was before Internet ads were popping up on everyone's portable electronic devices!

At first, you might say, "No way. That seems like an extremely high number." In reality, if we took a minute to consciously look for media and advertising messages during our day, we would see them everywhere. Bus stops, signs, storefronts, posters, magazines, cell phones, Instagram, Facebook, all other social-media forms, newspapers, billboards, TV, movies, commercials—it goes on and on. I live in Los Angeles, and just one drive to get lunch could jump my advertising messaging number up by hundreds. In fact, *The Guardian* did such an experiment in London using special eyeglasses and reported that a Londoner will typically see 3,500 messages in a day. Maybe when we consciously evaluate our surroundings, 5,000 messages per day isn't as outlandish as we initially thought. To quote one ad executive, J. Walker Smith: "The exact number may be hard to agree on, but it is an exponentially higher number with every passing decade."

It is interesting to me that whether we are consciously evaluating the advertisements we see each day or not, we still retain many of their messages. When we see an advertisement and consciously respond to it, then we are, by definition, using our conscious mind. However, we are exposed to many advertisements that we do not evaluate consciously, in which case the messaging and imagery get stored in our subconscious mind. Once stored in the subconscious, it has the ability to influence us.

The Pressure to Be Seen as Acceptable

To try to understand better where Freud was coming from with his theories, I took a closer look at what his society was like. Born in 1856 and living in Vienna from the time he was four, Freud grew up in a society that discouraged the public display of emotions like love and affection. In the late 1800s, Vienna was the capital of a far-flung empire under the rule of the Habsburg emperor, Franz Josef. However, after a long period of peace, the formal affluence that was seen on the surface was being challenged by a cultural, social, and economic change. Freud was one player in the unrest that threatened the strict order imposed by the established rulers and upper echelons of society. They did not welcome Freud's ideas because his line of thinking posed a threat to the rulers' control over the people. If people started to think and examine themselves, then before long they would also begin to examine their society, rulers, and so on. It is much easier to control large masses of people when they are following rules and regulations and not thinking outside of the box that has been provided for them to live in!

Understanding this, a lightbulb went off in my mind. It reminded me of some of my experiences and conversations with my grandparents. I have talked with them many times about what it was like when they were little. I have asked them, "Why is it so hard for you to show affection or even say, 'I love you'?" They explained to me that saying "I love you" was not something people did when they were growing up.

In the time that Freud lived and during my grandparents' generation, you were not allowed to show your feelings, such as sadness or love. Emotions, it was thought, made you vulnerable, and therefore showing them was viewed as a sign of weakness that would result in the lack of respect from others in your community. If you were viewed as weak and not well respected, then your place in society was threatened. This threatened your survival, which made it completely necessary to toe the line, which meant locking your emotions away deep inside.

When I stopped to think about this concept more, it made me wonder: If people are forced to look, act, and present themselves in ways that have been deemed "acceptable," then how much of themselves are they hiding? This led me to ask: How much of *myself* have I repressed in the fear of not being accepted and respected? Today we see examples of this more than ever through social media.

How many people do you personally know on Instagram or Facebook who present an image of themselves and their lives that is completely false? We've all seen this (and perhaps done it ourselves). We can name a list of people who present a completely false reality through social media in order to—what? Be accepted. It's easier for them to pretend to be what they think others want them to be than it is for them to show who they really are and risk rejection. I certainly understand why. Our society seems to have a lot in common with Freud's society in Vienna. People aren't allowed to be who they truly are because they will be targeted and ridiculed for being different.

I recently spoke to a freshman in high school who attended one of our body-image events. She shared the pressure she feels to be sexy and said, "Have you seen the kinds of photos that girls are posting online? I don't want to post pictures like that because it makes me feel uncomfortable, but those girls have the most followers and the guys like them."

Sadly, the message that young girls receive is that the number one way to get a following is to show skin and post sexy photos. In the past, it was marketing and advertising agencies alone that were behind sexualized images; now young girls themselves are creating and posting content that perpetuates the unhealthy belief that our looks determine how much love, happiness, and success we are entitled to.

Social media is a prime tool for seeking validation and acceptance, and in our digital age, one bad decision can go viral in seconds. Take, for instance, a story that Vincent, a 12-year-old boy, told me on a flight.

A seventh-grade girl at Vince's school had been pressured by two seventh-grade boys to take photos for them with her shirt off. The photos were sent around the school in a matter of minutes. I asked Vince what he thought about that. He said he felt really bad for the girl because everyone made fun of her and she got in trouble at school. Her phone was taken away as a punishment, while the two boys didn't receive any punishment at all. "I don't think that was right, because those boys were the ones who made her do it. It was their idea; then she got in trouble," he said. While this particular incident was relatively harmless, many other young people take their attempts at gaining approval to much greater extremes.

Becoming More Conscious

Since learning about the existence and nature of my conscious and subconscious minds, I am becoming more conscious! Meaning, I am more aware, more often, in the present moment, of the things I am being exposed to and how they contribute to what I think and feel about myself—things I would never have even noticed before! It is funny how that works. I realized that a huge part of my decision making and thought process was a product of my mind being on autopilot. In other words, I was not consciously questioning and analyzing the messages I was receiving like, in order to be "summer ready" and have a "bikini body," I need to diet and lose weight.

Logically that makes no sense. I have been on beaches around the world, and the thing I love the most about them is seeing all the different women having a wonderful time no matter what body type they have. Observing that in real life was proof that no one needs to lose weight to wear a bikini or get ready for summer. You also don't need to lose weight to go to the beach and have an amazing time, but we have accepted the belief that we do, and as a result we miss out on wonderful experiences. It was beliefs like this that I had accepted instead of analyzing and questioning them. Isn't it fascinating to realize that you are being controlled on a subconscious level while consciously believing that you are in complete control? How is that possible?

■ ■ ■

Advertising agencies are well aware of Freud's theories about human consciousness, as they have laid the foundation for the mass manipulation of human decision making by corporations. But it was Freud's nephew Edward Bernays who changed America from a "needs" to a "wants" society.

Using his uncle's theories, he developed strategies to sell products to the subconscious mind instead of the conscious mind. As the "father of public relations," Bernays pioneered manipulation to convert the masses into consumers, and this has everything to do with why you feel the way you do about your body and self-worth. We look at that next.

■ ■ ■ ■ ■

Chapter 5

Awakening to the
Media Manipulation

The fact that your subconscious mind influences your decision making might be news to you, but advertisers have known about it since the 1930s. That's right—all this time they have been using the principles of human psychology to manipulate consumers into buying products. Freud may have explained the workings of the subconscious mind, but it was his nephew Edward Bernays who applied his ideas to advertising. In fact, Bernays is the man responsible for the type of messages that dominate today's advertising.

Bernays was a very smart man who explored his uncle's theories about subconscious desires and realized the power they possessed. Recognizing the potential to play on people's irrational emotions instead of giving them rational information, he developed the advertising industry and coined the phrase *public relations*. Working with major corporations,

Bernays almost single-handedly transformed American culture from a "needs" to a "wants" system.

Ads to Control the Masses

Bernays didn't start his career promoting products. Born in Vienna in 1891, he moved with his family to New York City the following year. In his 20s, he worked for the U.S. government to gain public support for World War I by promoting the idea that it was a fight to bring democracy to Europe. When he accompanied Woodrow Wilson to the Paris Peace Conference, Bernays saw firsthand how propaganda made Wilson a hero to the masses. He began to realize that manipulating people's emotions, as individuals and as groups, was a means to control people in times of war and times of peace.

Heavily influenced by political columnist Walter Lippmann, Bernays determined that people were more likely to accept things that were presented as news rather than as advertising. In the 1920s, people still relied on newspapers for much of their information. He became skilled in obtaining newspaper coverage for wartime propaganda, using techniques such as the press release and the opinions of experts to influence people to rally behind a cause.

For example, in the campaign to rally support for Wilson's war policies, Bernays applied Freud's theories to create propaganda campaigns that tapped into the public's subconscious desires (such as to bring democracy to Europe) and subconscious emotions (such as pride and patriotism), instead of giving them facts with which to form an independent opinion. If he could get the public to act based on subconscious desires and emotions instead of thinking consciously based on facts, then he could create a movement behind whatever it was he wanted them to support. Was it honest? Perhaps not. Did it work? Yes!

When it comes to war and politics, selective news reporting and propaganda still exist today. For instance, during American elections, many TV ads say horrible things about opposing candidates. It's like mean-girl bullying on national TV, and I had never thought twice about it before. Then I realized I was being manipulated. This type of propaganda targets one candidate's character so that viewers will have a subconscious emotional reaction to that person and be swayed toward supporting the opponent. Meanwhile, I had no evidence to support the accusations that were made—and that is why this form of manipulation is so powerful. You don't need proof; you just need a belief—and oftentimes just hearing or reading something is enough for us to believe that it's true.

When leaders and politicians need public support to go to war, they need to make the public believe the war is necessary. In order to do that, the government may hide the true agenda for war and feed the public a story that it can rally behind. That is exactly what Edward Bernays did, and he was extremely successful in his efforts. Then, when World War I drew to a close, he focused on putting his strategies to other uses. During an interview late in his life, Bernays reflected on the time he realized that "if you could use propaganda for war, you could certainly use it for peace." Bernays began to study his uncle's theories and wondered how he could manipulate the subconscious to control the behavior of the urban masses. He established his office as a "public relations counselor" in New York City and before long was applying Freud's theories to sell products and make a lot of money. This is how our culture went from a "needs" to a "wants" system.

Is It a Need or a Want?

Throughout World War I, most Americans purchased something only if it was a necessity, a "need." Advertising focused on the practical virtues of a product. Although the wealthy could buy luxuries, the masses spent their money on things that would work and would last. Companies promoted their products by showing their practicality and durability. For example, one commercial from that time shows a woman selling ladies' hosiery. As she pulls the stocking over her hand and spreads her fingers out wide, she explains how durable and long lasting these stockings are. She is selling to women based on need and quality rather than image.

After the war ended, America's manufacturers started to produce consumer goods at an unprecedented rate; corporations were in fear of overproduction. If people purchased only what they needed, well, then you would hardly sell much at all. Bernays recognized that appealing to logic and need was greatly limiting sales. Bernays took an innovative approach— sell to people based on their wants rather than their needs.

If you can convince people that they should want an item even when they don't need it, you can drive consumption way up. A huge eye-opener for me was the story of how Bernays partnered with cigarette companies to get women to smoke. In the early 1900s it was not considered proper for women to smoke in public. Realizing that they were missing out on half of their potential customer base, the American Tobacco Company turned to Bernays for a solution.

Clearly there was no *need* for women to smoke, so Bernays met with a well-known psychoanalyst to learn what cigarettes meant to women, what might motivate them to buy them and light up. He discovered that, for women, cigarettes symbolized power. At that time, suffragettes had just recently won the right for women to vote in a male-dominated society. Bernays, the master of manipulation that he was, realized that if he could get women to believe that by smoking (considered a masculine act), they were more powerful and equal to men, then they would smoke.

Bernays staged a big media event in 1929 to manipulate women's perception of smoking. Bernays chose the huge Easter Parade in New York City as the perfect opportunity for his publicity stunt. He had invitations sent out by prominent feminist Ruth Hale, encouraging women to "light another torch of freedom." He also hired several beautiful socialites to attend the parade looking glamorous. He had countless connections with newspapers in Europe and was close friends with William Randolph Hearst, the owner of the largest chain of American papers, so he made sure that the press and local photographers would be in the right place at the right time.

At the event, on Bernays's cue, the socialites pulled out cigarettes that were hidden in their clothing and lit up. Cameras captured these beautiful women smoking unapologetically for all to see. The next day newspapers everywhere carried headlines about the "torches of freedom" and called it a bold protest for women's liberation. These images were printed around the world and became symbolic of the independent woman. Soon after, the sale of cigarettes to women rose dramatically, as did the profits of the cigarette companies.

When I learned about this, I sat at my computer with my mouth hanging open and almost fell out of my chair. How could he do that? It was a total lie! Not to mention he manipulated all these amazing women who were in support of female liberation to smoke. It wasn't liberation, it was manipulation.

Celebrity Sells

Bernays did not stop at publicity stunts like the "torches of freedom." He was the first person to do product placement, which entails stars wearing particular clothing or jewelry in the movies. Because Bernays's public relations firm represented movie stars and celebrities, he had the connections to get celebrities to say they use the products of his corporate clients. We see this kind of celebrity endorsement all the time. Often, the celebrities don't actually use the products they are selling, but because they are famous and people desire to be like them, the products will sell.

I often use the commercial that Justin Bieber did for the acne medication Proactiv in the Re-Model Me presentations I do at high schools because it is the perfect example of media manipulation. The commercial begins with Justin working in a recording studio. He says, "Hey, guys, Justin Bieber here. There are some things that just come with being a teenager. Your feet grow like crazy. I can't stop that. Your hormones kick in. I don't want to stop that. And then there are zits, and I *can* stop that. That's why I use Proactiv, because there is no way I'm gonna let a bunch of zits get in my way." The commercial then shows before and after images of people, apparently "real clients" who have perfect skin in the after photos (which we can't be sure were not just digitally altered with Photoshop or improved using makeup). It is clear that Justin Bieber never suffered from acne like the teens used as before and after examples.

The next scene is Justin playing basketball. He says, "I used to think that Proactiv was only for the hard-core cases. Guess what? It's also just right for kids like me." The commercial cuts to primarily teenage girls talking about how much the product changed their skin. By using Justin's celebrity with a huge fan base of teenage girls, Proactiv was able to say, "Use our product if you have acne—and even if you don't." If teenage girls see that Justin Bieber hates zits and he uses the product, they too will want to use the product. Subconsciously they want Justin Bieber's approval and to be seen as attractive. The boys watching the commercial would want to be like Justin, and so they subconsciously want the product in order to be more attractive to girls and to be successful like him. The media manipulates the public view: even when there is no "need" for a product, they can use a celebrity like Justin Bieber to create the "want."

Just as teenagers are persuaded by Justin, people of all ages tend to subconsciously trust a product more if it has physicians' approval. Bernays was the first to survey doctors to "recommend" products. One of the surveys he conducted was for eating bacon for breakfast! Doctors were even advocates of smoking Camels and Lucky Strikes. Even today people subconsciously trust a product more if the actor selling it on-screen is wearing a white lab coat and the advertisers say that the product has a physician's approval.

Who are these "doctors," "physicians," and "specialists"? We're rarely given a name (and when we are, there is generally a note on-screen that the individual has been compensated to appear in the ad). We are just told that top-level experts approve the item for sale. With the changes Bernays created in our consumer society, it's possible for corporations to no longer focus on creating good products and instead just package them well and sell them in a way that connects to consumers' subconscious desire to be loved and accepted.

In today's pop culture, celebrity is everywhere. You may not realize that whenever we see celebrities in the media, public relations is also usually involved. You know when you see a celebrity in a gossip magazine walking out of a store holding a product, coffee, or even grabbing a piece of gum?

There are many cases in which that was a product endorsement deal and they were paid to do that. We see this more than ever on social-media platforms. Celebrities, and now even fashion bloggers, post photos of themselves with a product and talk about how much they love it, when in reality they received a huge paycheck for that post.

So much of what is in today's media is fabricated and sensationalized and then sold to us as "reality." The result is that we are entertained but also that we end up desiring a life we believe is much better—more exciting and glamorous—than our own. If corporations can get us to have this mentality, they benefit immensely. If we are not buying things out of need but merely because we want them, and we are conditioned through media to believe we are not enough and will never have enough, then we will never stop consuming. Sadly, our self-image, society, and planet are suffering while corporations profit.

Tapping into Hidden Desires

Nearly every piece of advertising you see has the same underlying plan: to evoke a thought or emotion that subconsciously makes you more likely to purchase the product. That's why the adage "sex sells" is so true.

Some of my favorite examples of this point are advertisements for Axe body spray. Axe is a brand of grooming products targeting young men as their main consumer, so the marketing tactic is based around male sexuality. One commercial shows hordes of models in bikinis running in an animalistic manner, with boobs bouncing and intense looks on their faces (shot in slow motion, of course). Watching the commercial for the first time, you would have no idea what product it is actually for until the very end, when all the women find themselves at the same place—next to an average-looking, shirtless man who is smiling and applying Axe body spray. The ad campaign sends the message to young men that if they use Axe body spray, they will be irresistible to beautiful women. How realistic is that?

I started to look for other examples of this kind of messaging, which is often hidden. I remember seeing a commercial for Victoria's Secret with model Adriana Lima. She was wearing lingerie and wings, walking through hanging white drapes with her hair blowing in the breeze. The commercial was really short and just showed shots of her body and face looking glamorous and angelic. Adriana said, "The first time I put on wings, it felt very empowering. It was like a dream." When I saw that commercial, I thought something like, *She is so pretty. I am fat. Ugh, why can't I look like that? I am starting my diet Monday.*

But then I looked at the commercial more deeply. I took Adriana and myself out of the equation—because neither of us had a personal connection to the commercial or its message. Adriana was getting paid to show up and say her lines. The commercial was not her idea. And I personally had no relationship to the commercial or to the company. Victoria's Secret was the party with the vested interest: selling something. The question was, what were they selling?

We are aware that Victoria's Secret sells sexy lingerie, but is that what they were selling in that commercial? At first view you might say yes, because Adriana was wearing lingerie. Interestingly enough, there was no mention of the product at all. There was the image of her *in* the product but the only things mentioned were wings, empowerment, and a dream. Even without seeing the commercial, it is clear they were not selling you a bra, they were selling you empowerment. Or, at least, what they wanted you to believe was empowerment.

Remember the "torches of freedom"? The American Tobacco Company was selling "liberation" in the form of cigarettes—and Victoria's Secret was selling "empowerment" in the form of lingerie. The connections between the products (cigarettes/lingerie) and the states of being (liberation/empowerment) are completely irrational, but the tactic makes you wonder: What is it that women want, at their core? I think it is fair to say that all of us want to be empowered and liberated, right? Bernays and Victoria's Secret were appealing to these subconscious desires in us.

Freud said that there are desires in every human that we have stored away, often in the subconscious. That means that even if we aren't aware of them, those desires can be manipulated through media when advertisers tap into them in the attempt to sell products. I am very aware of my passion for women's rights and equality, but I would have never thought twice about the Victoria's Secret commercial selling the idea of being empowered by having wings on, wearing lingerie, and looking like Adriana Lima!

Even when the messaging is clear and right in front of us, because we have been manipulated and conditioned to accept media information as truth without processing and analyzing it, we often simply never notice what we are being told or sold. It wasn't until I learned about the "torches of freedom" that I was able to view media messaging with open eyes and a conscious mind and process the information rather than mindlessly store it in my subconscious. I still have moments when I think to myself, *I am an intelligent person. How could I have never even noticed this before?* I felt tricked and angry when I realized just how much power the media holds, and how that power is being used for monetary gain regardless of the negative effects on people and our society as a whole.

What Exactly Are We Being Sold through the Skinny Ideal?

After learning about Freud and Bernays and their effect on consumerism, it became clear to me that there is no logic to support our culture's skinny beauty ideal. This ideal is not healthy, realistic, or even attainable for most of us, and it is causing astronomical pain and self-loathing. It is time to find the hidden agenda of this ideal and ask ourselves what being skinny offers us. What does being skinny represent in our culture today?

When I ask girls and women this question, I can see them searching for an answer. "Beauty!" is usually the first response. Yes, being skinny is representative of beauty in our culture. But what else is it symbolic of? "Happiness!" is usually the next answer, followed by "popularity," "success," "empowerment," "acceptance," and "love." Do you ever see advertising images of women eating salads or taking diet pills in which they are *not* laughing and smiling? Of course not, because—didn't you know?—happiness comes with being thin.

The media tends to show two extremes—being ultra-thin or being extremely large. In real life, there is a spectrum of sizes, with the majority fitting somewhere in the middle. That middle ground is virtually nonexistent in the entertainment and fashion industries. Because of that, we have one-dimensional female characters who are not representative of real women. Every advertisement you see that uses professional models is promoting the idea that being tall and thin is better. If you look like them, then you will have the happiness, acceptance, beauty, popularity, empowerment, and love you are searching for. When girls and women attend my Re-Model Me events and we reach this point in the presentation, I can actually see the wheels in their minds start to turn.

Is it fair to say that every woman desires to be beautiful, happy, successful, empowered, accepted, and loved? I know I want those things. It is clear that in our subconscious minds, we share these desires. Psychoanalysts and advertising agencies are well aware of this. The purpose of the beauty ideal is to be symbolic of these desires. The reason for creating an image that connects you to your subconscious desires is to influence your opinion of any given product. When the image of the beauty ideal is connected with products that you don't necessarily need, you will be convinced you *want* those products. Subconsciously, you believe that if you buy the products, you can look like the beauty ideal and thus fulfill your true desires—to be beautiful, happy, successful, empowered, accepted, and loved. Of course, this doesn't work!

Unattainable for a Reason

We have covered why the beauty ideal exists—to create a connection between products we don't need and qualities, values, and attributes we want. Now I would like to take a closer look at the *need* for our beauty ideal to be unattainable. It is no accident that beauty ideals are unattainable; it makes perfect sense in the world of consumerism and leads us right back to the needs vs. wants system.

What happens when we are unable to attain a dream? When we want something we have not yet achieved, we either continue to pursue it or feel like a failure for not having achieved it. In the process, we might buy products to help us attain our dream. If we reach our goals, we stop striving for it. We stop our consumption of products. Think about how this idea applies to the pursuit of the beauty ideal. If we were to attain the beauty ideal, we would stop spending money on diet tea, diet pills, waist trainers, and quick-fix products.

When corporations promote an unattainable ideal, it is to guarantee we will never stop trying to be like the ideal—and shelling out cash in the process.

The irony, of course, is that even if we reach the beauty ideal physically, we do not receive the fulfillment we were promised—happiness, success, empowerment, and love. We are left with the fear of losing what we've got, because we believe that without it, we are not enough—so we continue to consume products in our obsession to maintain the ideal.

Why Do We Accept It?

We know this ideal is not offering anything positive to women or to society, so why do we accept it? Why don't we question it? I have thought about this a lot. As women, when we are operating under the fear of being unlovable, we are disconnected from our true selves and one another. We are so consumed with the image of who we need to be that we become separate from who we really are. We focus all of our energy, thoughts, and time on obtaining an unachievable goal.

For many of us, that goal is losing weight and being as beautiful as possible so that we can be of value. When we are solely focused on transforming our physical bodies into society's beauty ideal, we are disconnected from our souls. We are not learning more about ourselves on a soul level. We are not learning more about our purpose and why we are here. Regardless of how we look on the outside, we are empty and numb on the inside.

When we fill our minds with these ideas and beliefs and don't nourish our bodies, we are not capable of seeing the hidden agenda. We are not strong enough in mind and spirit to challenge these beliefs and choose not to accept them.

When I finally asked myself who was trying to keep me small and why, I began to understand. A strong body nourishes a healthy mind. A healthy body and mind provide oxygen for the fire that lives in our soul.

Ellyn Silverman, one of HNS's nutrition experts who works with girls recovering from eating disorders, said something to me that really clicked. "When you are in an unhealthy place and you are not nourishing your body, you cannot expect to have a healthy mind and soul. Our mind, body, and soul are connected and one affects the other. If you are not nourishing your body, you are not nourishing your mind. If you are not in a healthy place with your mind or your body, then your soul will suffer." I realize now that part of the reason I never questioned the beauty ideal was because my body was not well nourished, and because of that my mind was weak. That kept me unconscious of what I was doing—always searching for things outside of myself to fulfill me on the inside, which perpetuated my disconnection from my true self and my true source of self-love: my soul.

We have so many wonderful things to offer the world. Each one of us has passions and gifts that can bring light to our too-dark world. The fire that lives in the female spirit cannot burn, however, when its oxygen source has been cut off. Every form of media has an agenda. Too many magazines brainwash us into buying into a lifestyle that comes with countless products the magazines are paid to promote. Fashion and beauty magazines occupy our thoughts with superficial ideas that keep us shallow and simpleminded. We need content that challenges our thinking, and to be praised and celebrated for being successful in arenas other than physical beauty.

We have been manipulated into starving our bodies, minds, and souls in the pursuit of the one thing we desire most—to be accepted and loved. That is why no matter how hard we try to feel better, we can't be fulfilled, because we believe that our bodies need to be "fixed" first! The truth is that there is nothing wrong with your body. You were not created to live your life weak and small. You were created with a beautiful essence, and your body is your vessel for sharing your light with the world.

Getting to the Heart of My Own Self-Loathing

When I started to take a closer look at myself and really examine some of the feelings that had dominated so much of my life, I became aware that I had been operating on self-loathing and self-hatred that was caused by my desire—and failure—to be like the beauty ideal. Because I fell short, my overall view of myself was that I was not good enough. My body was never good enough. I was not small enough in either real life or the straight-size modeling world, and in the plus-size modeling world, there were people who felt I was not large enough. I couldn't escape the opinions others had of my body and how I "should" look to be acceptable. I never felt as though my photos were good enough. I would look at each one and see flaws and ugliness. I was motivated by an overwhelming sense of disgust when I looked at myself in the mirror. I didn't want to tell people I was a model because I knew they would look at my size and think, *You couldn't be a model. You are too fat!*

All of these thoughts would play in my mind without my even realizing it. It was the subconscious soundtrack to my life. It wasn't until I stopped to examine the thoughts and really listen to them that I realized something was seriously wrong. The upsetting feelings I had about myself finally triggered my conscious mind to stop and question my thoughts, beginning with, *How could I be so horrible to myself?* I would never say those things to another person, so why did I think I deserved that kind of abuse?

I realized, to my surprise, that *so much* of my life had been focused on beauty and body image in various ways. Most of the time, my experiences pertaining to and my relationship with my body were toxic. But then there were some empowering and uplifting experiences, as well. I would have days, weeks, sometimes months where I felt really strong and confident. Then I would have a day, week, or month when I would look in the mirror and just feel unattractive, fat, and gross. If I ever vocalized these feelings, I would get absolutely zero empathy from anyone because I was a model and therefore not allowed to be a human being with feelings about my appearance like everyone else. Why did I believe that my size meant I was disgusting or somehow unlovable? Where and when did I develop that program?

The one thing I just could not understand was why so much of my life had involved a constant struggle to feel good about myself. Why couldn't the good feelings and experiences last? I know that we cannot feel good *all* the time—that's not realistic as human beings. But why were my positive feelings fleeting while my negative feelings seemed to be the foundation of my being? And why did I believe only the negative things people said about me, disregarding all the amazing things they said? So many times I'd felt as though I would make such great progress and then fall right back to where I started when it came to appreciating what I saw in the mirror and liking myself. Why?

People often assume that models must be very secure with their looks, but I think being a model actually heightens your insecurities because you are constantly being judged on your appearance. Not only your livelihood but also your self-worth hinges on how "picture perfect" you are at any given time. I realize now that models feel exactly the same way as girls who wish to be models. We are all searching for something to fulfill us and make us feel okay.

The girls who dream of becoming a model feel that if they do, they will be happy, important, loved, and fulfilled. The girls who model for a living believe that if they can be skinnier and more beautiful, and book bigger campaigns, then they will be happy, important, loved, and fulfilled. We all do the same harmful things to our bodies to achieve these goals. We are all searching for something external to make us whole on the inside, and yet we always seem to fail.

How can so many girls strive to be beautiful like models, and yet the models themselves don't feel beautiful? How is it possible that there has been a beauty ideal created that guarantees all girls and women will fail? Even if you physically achieve the ideal, if you are harming your body in the process and can't see your own beauty, are you really succeeding?

My Game Changer and Yours

Meeting my now husband, Bradford, was a game-changing experience for me with this pattern of self-loathing and negative self-talk and beliefs. He was the "pattern interrupt" I needed to jolt me out of my self-destructive mind-set and help me go back to zero, to square one, where I could let go of the false beliefs I had built my self-image and self-esteem on and start all over again, this time thinking and questioning and determining what was true for me.

I was at a Christmas party with a friend, and when I saw Bradford walk in, I immediately thought to myself, *Holy shit, that guy is beautiful.* He was tall, dark, and handsome, with an amazing smile. Obviously that meant I couldn't look at him!

I pretended to look at other things and was caught off guard when he was suddenly standing right next to me introducing himself. He was really friendly. We talked about how he was from Missouri and I was from Wyoming. There was a nice connection between us. He asked me what I did for a living, and I reluctantly said, "I am a plus-size model."

"I don't know what that means," he said, "and I don't want you to take this the wrong way . . ." (At that point I braced for him to finish with something offensive.) "I saw you as soon as I walked in here," he continued, "and you are honestly the most beautiful woman I have ever seen. I don't know what a plus-size model is, but I would just say that it sounds pretty perfect. I started in the industry as a fitness model and have done runway shows for a long time, and seeing how thin some of these girls are is concerning. When I work runway shows, the male and female models have to change in the same area at times. I have seen the girls bend over and you can see every bone in their bodies. It is not healthy. So please don't think I am a creep. I just want you to know that you are perfect, and don't let this messed-up industry tell you otherwise."

I was speechless because that was the last thing I expected him to say. My negative, self-loathing mind would never have thought this nice, charming, attractive man would say something so genuinely sweet about me. At that stage in my life, it was impossible for me to allow myself the possibilities of good things, nice people, and happiness, because I had already convinced myself that I was not good enough to deserve any of them.

Thank God I accepted Bradford's invitation to go on a date the following evening and didn't let my insecurity cause me to back out. We had an amazing time and stayed up all night talking and laughing, which we still do to this day. Bradford played an important role for me at that point in my life. He challenged the negative views I had of myself because he didn't agree with them at all. His contradicting what I believed about myself and the beauty ideal helped me step back and see things more objectively. It was a turning point for me as, little by little, I started to challenge other beliefs, as well.

That is what I hope to do for you with this book—to act as your pattern interrupt, your "Bradford," helping you see that *you are beautiful*; you just don't see yourself accurately yet, mainly because you are so busy comparing yourself with an outwardly imposed, narrow, unattainable, and unrealistic beauty ideal. Like me, you need to start asking yourself why you don't already have a clear sense of your true worth. I actually think that we all once did, but we lost it as life inundated us with messages to the contrary.

■ ■ ■

Knowledge *is* power. Now you know some important things about the Western beauty ideal—where it comes from (advertisers), why it exists (to make money off us), and what it does (makes us feel bad about ourselves). You may not realize it yet, but you are strong enough to reject the false dream of being or looking like a model—and to replace it with your *real* dream, the one that arises from your true self and is not imposed on you by society. This may sound huge—and it is. But don't worry. In upcoming chapters, I will guide you step by step through the process of taking your power back.

In Part II of this book, I want to help you take what you're learning and begin to apply it to your own life. I want to help you wake up to the media messaging that is constantly bombarding you, and to look for the agenda in its imagery and messages. I want to help you learn how to take your power back from those who have their bottom line rather than your highest good at heart. I want to empower you to become the gatekeeper as to what messages get into your mind, influencing how you think and feel about yourself, as this will affect the actions you take every moment of every day and thus the life that you ultimately create.

I won't lie to you. The path to reconnecting with your body, mind, and soul is a long and arduous one that covers a unique landscape for each of us. Yet it is the most meaningful and fulfilling journey we can take in life.

■ ■ ■ ■ ■

Part Two

WHAT YOU
CAN DO TO FEEL
BETTER NOW

Chapter 6

Big Girl in a Skinny World

Once I learned about Freud and Bernays, I wanted to reconstruct what messaging I might have been exposed to in the past and see if I could discern how it had affected me. What programming had been pouring into my mind since a young age? What beliefs had it caused me to develop about myself, others, and the world? What decisions had it influenced?

Looking back, I realized that much of my self-loathing stemmed from being a "big girl in a skinny world." I had accepted the belief that I was "lesser than"; I had accepted disappointment, letdowns, negativity, an unhealthy lifestyle, and shallow friends because that was what I thought was normal and all I deserved. It was very freeing to identify my foundational beliefs and realize that they didn't belong to me.

That gave me the permission I needed to not have to buy into them anymore.

Just in case no one's told you, let me say it here: *You're a good person who deserves a good life.* I'd like to help you achieve that. It starts with becoming aware of how you are being programmed from the outside, then reclaiming the territory of your own mind. To regain your sense of self-worth, you need to go back to the beginning, as I did, and start fresh. You'll need to wipe the slate clean of all the false beliefs that have been programmed into you. You'll need to find out why you ever stopped loving yourself.

To help you begin looking back through your own life history, I'll share with you some of the things I discovered in my own.

Going Back to Zero

I love to watch really little kids play because they are so unaware of what they look like; actually, they are unaware of pretty much everything. Kids are special because they don't give two thoughts about what people think about them, what is going on around them, or what they look like, because they are too busy being free, joyful, excited, and happy. They don't live in the future or past; they are truly present in each moment. When I think about my childhood and connect to my very young, happy, unaware self, several memories come to mind.

I remember going to some botanical gardens with my mom and older brother, Evan. We didn't really do anything but sit and play on a wooden swing. Sometimes we would get a burrito and take it for lunch. The gardens were quiet and smelled like flowers. A feeling of peacefulness comes over me whenever I think about it.

Another favorite memory is when I was about five years old and Evan and I decided to play hide-and-seek. I had the genius idea to hide in my wicker clothes hamper that had an elephant head as a lid. Well, I didn't just hide in the hamper. Oh no, I was too clever for that. I pulled the clothes out first, then got in and put the clothes back on top of me, followed by the lid. The best part was I could see out of the hamper perfectly and would know when my brother came in the room looking for me. Sure enough, he came in and looked under the bed and in the closet, and I remember trying not to make a sound as he walked toward the hamper. He took off the lid, and I thought for sure I was found, but then he put the lid back on and ran out of the room to continue searching.

I remember thinking, *I have found the best hiding spot in the entire world!* I was so proud of myself. I just sat there dead silent and waited this one out. After about 30 minutes, my brother yelled, "Okay, I give up. Come out. The game is over!" I was convinced that this was just a trick to get me to come out so he could say, "Found you!" I wasn't going to fall for that, so I stayed hidden. When my mom couldn't find me and I refused to come out even after they had repeatedly shouted that the game was over, my mom (I found out later) began to think I had been kidnapped.

After about an hour and a half of sitting in my hamper, I could tell that my mom and brother had left the house, so I went outside laughing, full of excitement because I had won. I had outsmarted everyone, and it was a sweet victory! As soon as my mom saw me out there, she grabbed me and hugged me so hard it hurt. Tears ran down her face. She asked where I had been, and, when I told her, she was so upset she spanked me! Then hugged me, then spanked me, and told me to never do that again. This memory has stayed with me for so long because I remember being so confused and yet truly proud of myself, even after being spanked, for being so smart.

The memory is a great example of how as kids we can be unaware and free from self-consciousness. I wasn't just unaware of my looks and body, I was completely unaware of everything and everyone other than what I was doing in that exact moment. It never occurred to me that my family would think I'd been kidnapped. I was just excited to win at hide-and-seek.

We're Born Loving Ourselves

When I recall times like these, I can see that I once did love myself. The self-love I remember was a feeling of comfort and contentment, of freedom and joy. It was not connected to my looks or my body in any way. The simple things made me feel loving toward myself. For example, I loved lollipops, and so I have tons of photos of me with lollipop juice all over my face. My hair was always crazy because I hated to brush it, and I remember feeling happy and carefree even with a rat's nest sitting on my head. I never let anyone dress me; I had to pick out my own clothes and would only wear things I liked. My outfits would be a random mixture of prints and colors along with mismatched socks and shoes, but I loved it! Whether I was playing in my room, riding my bike, or roller-skating around the house, I was pretty content with myself. I didn't mind being alone and was secure with who I was.

It is important to realize that every single one of us is born loving who we are. Babies are simple. For the first six months, they need food, sleep, love, and their diapers changed, and then you can add entertainment to the list for the next year or so as they retain information and learn from their environment. They laugh and cry as a way to communicate their needs. When you think back to your very early self, before you started to become aware of what was "wrong" with you, what do you remember feeling? What made you happy? What did you love to do?

And when did your self-contentedness fade away, replaced by its opposite?

Why Do We Stop?

I felt secure and loved as a child because I was in an environment that was secure and loving. But not everyone is so fortunate. In my work with Healthy Is the New Skinny, I have talked with countless girls and women who were happy as children, too, until things took a toxic turn. Many were victims of abuse and neglect, which took them from a natural state of security and love to self-loathing and fear. It has become clear to me that self-love is natural, and self-loathing is learned.

I wanted to understand why I had stopped loving myself. To find this answer, I really had to search my memories and spend time thinking about experiences that left a negative imprint on my spirit. I recalled several events that played a key role in the transition of my carefree, secure, self-loving self into my self-conscious, self-loathing, insecure self. As I looked back at my childhood, I could see that I stopped loving myself when I became aware of what other people thought of me. That awareness taught me to compare myself with others and to search for a place where I fit in. It was that early programming that developed the subconscious belief that to be worthy of my own acceptance, I needed to be accepted by others first.

Larger than Life

Sometimes I feel like I am just larger than the world around me. My mind works and thinks in "big-picture" ideas. I also feel big in the sense that I can flex and squeeze my arms together in front of me, ripping the seam down the back of whatever jacket or top I am wearing at any given moment! I have a big personality, strong spirit, and really broad shoulders. I identify with the scene from the 1995 movie *Tommy Boy* in which the late Chris Farley puts on David Spade's jacket, swings his arms back and forth singing "fat guy in a little coat," and splits the garment down the back. The thought of it makes me laugh because I feel as if it is a metaphor for my life in so many ways.

I've recently entered my 30s, but it wasn't until just a few years ago that I actually began to feel comfortable in my body. I didn't think I was unattractive; I just felt uncomfortable with my body and my size. I felt as though people viewed me as "the big girl," and in our culture being big is a horrible offense. It seemed, my whole life, everything had to do with size. I was always taller and larger than other girls. When it came to sports, this was a "deal maker," but when it came to popularity, hotness, and boys in general, it always seemed to be a "deal breaker." I learned that not being petite, small, or skinny as a girl was viewed as unattractive. But if you're lucky enough to have a pretty face, then there is always hope for you if you can just "fix" your body.

When my career in modeling started, I was 17, five nine, 182 pounds, and size 12. It was an interesting experience to add "plus-size model" to my identity as a "big girl." I wasn't really sure how I felt about it because, on one hand, I was so excited to model; on the other, I was totally embarrassed because I felt as though the label meant "fat." Even worse, I feared that other people would think that, too. After booking my first modeling job and receiving my day rate of $2,000, I didn't really care what people called me—or at least that's what I told myself.

Growing Up Different

Being tall as a child and preteen, the comment I would hear the most was, "Wow, she is so big." I was never aware of my size being abnormal or different until other people began making comments about it. I went from feeling content and secure with myself to being aware that I was not like everyone else. Even as a toddler I was always larger than everyone else my age, but I wasn't actually overweight until I was about eight years old. I am not sure why, but I started gaining weight, and by the time I was 10, I was at least 30 pounds overweight. I was called fat and ugly like every other kid who doesn't fit the beauty ideal. I was well aware that I was different, but I had no idea why or how to change it.

I was also raised with two beautiful cousins who were close in age but about half my size. They wore matching outfits, and I was unable to fit into the same clothing. They would always receive compliments from others about how cute and beautiful they were, while I never did. Experiences like these at such a young age reinforced the beliefs I was learning from some members of my family and other adults. I believed I was unattractive and developed a feeling of shame about my body and height because of verbal and nonverbal messaging that reinforced the belief that "I am not good enough."

In the fifth grade, I moved to Casper, Wyoming, away from the constant comparisons to my cousins and into a new beginning for me. I went to a smaller elementary school, which was nice; I knew everyone and could make friends more easily. When I went into the seventh grade, I started playing volleyball and basketball, which was a great way to stay active. I grew about five inches over the next two years and went to a healthier weight. With competitive sports, I felt I had finally found where I fit in. For the first time in my life, my height and size were viewed as a positive.

This feeling of fitting in didn't last very long. Things changed for me yet again when my brother moved to Nebraska to attend college, and Mom and I moved back to Washington when I was a sophomore in high school. After only a year of marriage, my mom had divorced my stepdad and had gotten a job offer back near my family in Spokane. I wasn't able to drive yet, so when I wasn't playing sports, I was always stuck at home. My mom worked full-time, so I fell back into the habit of eating for comfort and out of boredom. Of course, with these habits, I put on weight.

"N for 'Not Good Enough'"

Not only did I come in a package that was different from other girls my age, but also I acted differently. I have always had a strong sense of self, and, no matter what age I was, I always felt as though my opinions and ideas mattered. I viewed myself as an equal to anyone. As you might imagine, I did not respond well to authority figures who did not treat me with respect or would force me to do things I did not want to do.

To make matters worse, I had a difficult time in school and didn't learn how to read until the third grade. Turns out I am dyslexic and, because my brain function is dominant on my right side, I am extremely visual, which made it difficult to learn in the traditional way. After being tested in school, it was discovered that my IQ was high, but my reading and spelling abilities were low. I felt frustrated being in an environment that didn't teach me in a way that I could understand. I started to feel like I was dumb and there was something wrong with me. For part of each day, I had to go to a classroom where the "special kids" would go to learn. That in itself is shameful for young kids. You are separated from your peers for being different.

My second-grade teacher was a mean-spirited woman who would do things like make my classmate with a horrible stutter narrate the school play. She seemed to get joy out of humiliating kids, and unfortunately I was on her list. One time we had to take a reading and spelling test in class, which I was not supposed to participate in unless my tutor was there to assist me. But my teacher made me do the test on my own. I failed miserably, and she had me wait after class to meet with her. I remember feeling scared as I sat there and she showed me the test. She had written the letter *N* on it and circled it in red.

"Do you know what that means?" she asked me.

I shook my head.

"When you fail a test you get an F," she said.

I sat there, a confused second grader with no clue what she was talking about.

"The alphabet goes A, B, C, D. A is the best grade you can get, and F means you failed. I gave you an N, because you did worse than an F. You get an N for 'not good enough.'"

She then told me that I would need to try harder. My spirits were dashed, and I had a horrible feeling in my stomach. I couldn't help but cry because I *had* tried. After that experience I started to refuse to go to school. When my mom found out what was going on, she went to the principal immediately, took me out of that school, and got me transferred to a new one. In a much more positive environment at the new school, I was happier and learned to read.

But the damage had been done. I knew school was not a safe environment for me, and I did everything I could to not have to go. Some days my mom had to physically carry me out of the house in my pajamas and take me to school because I refused to get up or change my clothes. As my frustration grew with the environment I was forced to be in, my behavior became more wild and rebellious. I went from being a happy, carefree, secure girl to a "big troublemaker with a learning disability." Nothing had changed other than I had become aware of what others thought of me, and I had accepted the labels they gave me.

The Model Search

I believe I was in the third grade when I heard about modeling for the first time. My two cousins were excited because they were going to go to a model search that they'd heard about on the radio. I didn't really know what that was, but since they were going, I wanted to go, too!

They were tiny, adorable little girls and I was, well, me. At that point, I was well into my chubby, awkward phase. My favorite outfit was a floral bodysuit with a sewn-in lace vest and a classic French braid to top off my look. Being only nine, I was unable to grasp the concept of going to a model search and being judged on my looks and size; I just assumed that I would be joining everyone for this exciting event that they had all been talking about.

When the model search weekend rolled around, no one said a thing. I am pretty sure my aunts were hoping I would forget about it, but of course I asked my mom why they didn't pick me up to go with them. God love her, Mom did her best to spin it so that I wouldn't get my feelings hurt. She said that the people at the model search only liked one type of beauty, that they didn't represent all types, and she didn't think it was a good idea to be part of something like that. I may have been nine, but I wasn't completely naive; it was pretty clear that my aunts didn't want to take me because they knew I wouldn't be picked.

From this hurtful experience, I retained more programming to support the belief that being myself was wrong in some way or not good enough. It was around this time that my emotional connection to food got much stronger. I began eating when I wasn't hungry. I would eat alone because I knew that what I was doing was somehow wrong or shameful. I don't think I really understood what I was doing; I just knew it made me feel better. I felt comforted when I would hide at my grandparents' house and eat bags of popcorn alone.

My cousins, by the way, did get chosen and started to model. They booked jobs for JCPenney and a few other department stores. That lasted just a few years because both of them grew to be only five feet, and to model as an adolescent and adult you need to be at least five nine. Ironically, just as the model search made me feel inadequate because I did not fit what the judges were looking for, after having some success, my cousins ended up feeling the same way a few years later.

Still Too Big

In high school, I dated the same guy for three years. He was five ten—only one inch taller than I was. For some reason, girls really struggle with being as tall as or taller than boys. I always felt really big because I weighed more than my boyfriend. He ate fast food and junk food all the time, but it didn't affect his weight at all. He would just burn right through it. I did not have the same metabolism. Depending on my athletic schedule, I would go up and down in weight because, whether I was very active during the sports seasons or very inactive during our seasons off, my eating habits stayed the same. My boyfriend was a really nice guy, and we had so much fun together. I knew that he loved me for me and that my weight was not something he cared about. But I also knew that his friends were not nice like he was.

His friends would make fun of us because they were jealous that he would rather hang out with me than spend time with them. So I became a target at times for them to be mean to and try to bring down. As an adult I can totally see that this really had nothing to do with me; it was that I had broken up a "bro-mance" between my boyfriend and his best friend. Therefore, I was the enemy. The go-to words for shaming young women in our society is to call them fat, ugly, or a slut. I couldn't really be called a slut because I was only with my boyfriend, and I was not ugly by the boys' standards, but they could go with "fat."

I remember asking my boyfriend why he would want to hang around guys who were so immature and mean. His best friend in particular was always getting into trouble and treating girls horribly. I couldn't understand what the basis of their friendship was, because my boyfriend was not like that at all. "We have been friends forever. That is just the way he is," was the response he would give me.

There is one event that I will remember forever. My boyfriend and I went to different high schools, and he wanted me to go with him to his school's dance. While I was really excited to go, I felt a little uncomfortable because we would be going with a group of his guy friends and their dates. I didn't really like any of the guys, and I wouldn't know any of the girls. Nevertheless, I agreed to go and found an amazing dress for the dance. When I put it on, I felt so beautiful because it fit and flattered my size 12 body to perfection. I always did my own hair and makeup for dances because it was something I loved to do. I decided to go with wavy hair and simple makeup.

I showed up to his house for photos, and he looked as handsome as ever. Neither of us was a big fan of dances, but this one felt special and we were both excited. We stopped at the school for photos before heading to dinner with his friends. As we pulled into the school parking lot, a group of girls who knew my boyfriend waved and said hi. We didn't think anything of it and went into the school to shoot our photos.

At the restaurant, the girls in the group were not being welcoming, or even talking to me, for that matter. I excused myself to go to the restroom, and when I came back, I noticed my boyfriend acting really strange. His mood was a combination of mad, uncomfortable, and annoyed. I asked him what was wrong, and he wouldn't tell me. A horrible sense of insecurity came over me. I felt as if everyone else was in on a joke that no one bothered to tell me.

After I asked my boyfriend over and over why he was acting so odd, he finally told me what happened. When I had gone to the restroom, one of the girls came over to talk to him. She said, "When we saw you and your girlfriend pull up in your car, we thought, 'Wow, she is so pretty.' But then she got out. We had no idea she was so big."

I am not sure what hurt my feelings more, the fact that this girl whom I didn't even know was talking crap about me to my boyfriend, or that my boyfriend didn't defend me. I had started the night feeling so beautiful and happy, but I ended up feeling like a fat, undeserving embarrassment. As an adult, I can see that the girl probably liked my boyfriend and was jealous of me, so she tried to bring me down and ruin my evening. Well, she did! I decided that I just wanted to go home, and we skipped the dance altogether.

Experiences like this one caused deep feelings of shame, embarrassment, and the belief that I was not good enough. Even though I had a boyfriend who loved me, and I knew he loved me, I still had the fear that I was not worthy of love. I feared being fat and unattractive, and when it came to relationships, I feared that I would never be enough. I feared that I would ultimately end up sad and alone.

What I understand now is that it was never my body I was uncomfortable with. That is just what I had been made to believe. It was *me* who I didn't like. I wasn't comfortable with who I was as a person—mainly because I had no clue who I was. I had never taken the time to think about it much because I was consumed with images of who I "should" be, and how I "should" look. Even if other people didn't view me as "the big girl," it didn't matter because, after a while, I viewed myself that way. I projected my thoughts and insecurities onto those around me regardless of what they were actually thinking. My mind was on autopilot, subconsciously telling myself I was big and fat and therefore worthless. I was like a zombie in a way because I would mindlessly walk around with this sound loop ("I'm the big girl") playing over and over in my mind without being consciously aware of it.

■ ■ ■

In this chapter I shared with you some of the more memorable milestones in the process by which I detached from the moorings of my true self—the version of me that was born loving myself and felt at home in my body and in life. I described how I slipped into an abyss of insecurity as I tried to navigate a world where, according to its ideals, I would never be enough.

Now I invite you to do the same very important work. Reflect on your past: Where and when did you stop loving yourself? The strides you make now in tracking it back, despite the pain of recalling, will be powerful steps in your journey home to a place of self-loving and inner peace.

In Chapter 7, we examine the negative messaging we receive not when we're out in the world but when we're at home, with our own families.

■ ■ ■ ■ ■

Chapter 7

Examine the Messages You Received at Home

It is difficult growing up in a culture that is extremely judgmental and increasingly superficial; as we have seen, the media bombards young people with negative messaging. That is why it is so wonderful that we all have such loving families who counteract the negativity with positive reinforcement and love, supporting us in being who we are as individuals—right? While the idea is nice, it is often not a reality. We can agree that it is how it *should* be, but, unfortunately, we as children are not the only ones who suffer from societal expectations and media messaging.

We grow up thinking that our parents know better and we should respect them as authorities, but our parents and other family members fall victim to the same systems we do. Sometimes, even with the best of intentions, parents are wrong. To see our loved ones as they really are, with their human flaws and vulnerabilities, can be difficult. We don't want to think they might act in a way that hurts us, even unintentionally.

Every one of us is running on programming, like a computer's operating system. What varies is the type. When you have positive, healthy thoughts and feel good from the inside out, you run efficiently. But all it takes is one little virus to slow your operating system down and allow other "bugs" or negative beliefs about yourself to crash your computer. When the people you love the most in the world criticize and shame you for being who you are, it can really crush your spirit. To help you start to examine this part of your life, I will share some stories of negative programming from my own family.

Unconscious Beliefs

As I mentioned, my grandmother runs on very outdated programming from her childhood, where she learned that saying "I love you" was not acceptable. She developed the belief that if you are given food and a roof over your head, then you are loved. It is no surprise that she then raised her four daughters and son with this same belief. It wasn't until her grandchildren came around that her programming was challenged.

My mother developed a lot of negative beliefs about herself from my grandparents' old-fashioned programming. My grandparents were raised as strict Irish Catholics. My grandfather grew up extremely poor on the streets of South Boston and later joined the military. They never told my mother or my aunts that they were beautiful, and when I asked my grandmother why, she said, "Well, we didn't want them to be promiscuous." What? Why would telling your daughters they are beautiful lead them to sleep with every guy in town? You would think that if they felt beautiful and of value, the likelihood of their seeking validation from an outside source like random guys would be lower.

When I said these things to my grandmother, it was as though they had never occurred to her before. She never logically assessed these beliefs; she just said them and believed them because, well, that was what people told her would happen! She still says really hurtful things at times as a result of these unconscious beliefs. I often challenge my grandmother because unless she becomes aware of them, they will not change.

It is important to realize that children receive both verbal and nonverbal messaging. My mom told me that when I was six, I asked my grandma straight up, "How come you don't love me as much as you love Jessica and Adri?" (They were my two cousins who were my age.) My grandmother was shocked and looked at my mom wide-eyed, not knowing what to say. My mom said to her, "Answer the question." My grandmother said, "Oh, don't be ridiculous. Of course I love you the same."

But the truth came out years later when I invited my grandparents to stay with my husband and me in Mexico for a week. We got into a great debate! I am not kidding when I tell you that my grandmother said in her Boston accent: "Kate, the reason I didn't like you when you were little is because you were always causing trouble. I remember this one time I had gone to visit you guys when you were about five. We had a great day at the beach. You had on a little sweat-suit jumper thing, and you decided you wanted to go play in the watah. Now, I said, 'Do not get wet!' You didn't listen and were playing in the watah and sand with your sweatpants on. You had sand all ova the place. Now, we had plans to go to dinner, so we went back to the hotel and

I told you to change your pants. You said, 'No, I like these. I don't want to change.' I said, 'Now listen here, Kate, you are going to change your pants and that is it. There is sand all ova them and they are wet. We can't go to dinner like that!' You refused to change your pants and put up a big fuss, crying and kicking. We couldn't go to dinner because you wouldn't change your pants. You did things like that all the time, causing trouble. That is why people didn't like you then."

Clearly, playing in the sand was a horrible offense for a five-year-old. So while my grandmother hadn't said anything out loud, as a six-year-old, I was not far off in my understanding. I laughed as I told my mom the story, and she responded, "Welcome to my life."

My grandmother was raised in a time when, for women, having a husband was the most important thing in life. You were to look beautiful, be compliant, and present yourself as the perfect housewife. Then, if you got a guy, your next job was to keep him! Being slim was always expected of women; back then, the ideal just reflected different proportions than today's skinny ideal. The things my grandmother would say to my mom and aunts would be considered body shaming, bullying, and cruel today. But in her mind, my grandmother thought she was helping them—doing it "for their own good"! If only she could get them to see how fat they were and how they just needed to lose some weight, then they would get a husband and be taken care of.

I still work to broaden my grandmother's understanding of people and love. I don't get my feelings hurt anymore by the things she says because I know her programming is so out-of-date that it does not apply to me or to today's society. This allows me to love her for who she is while I continue to be myself and love myself for who I am.

Unlovable

In high school, my mom appeared to have it all, but inside she was empty and unfulfilled. She was the head cheerleader and prom queen, and she was dating my dad, who was the prom king and an all-star football, baseball, and basketball player. I have a photo of my mom from when she was in high school, and she was petite with amazing, muscular legs and big boobs. Whenever my mom sees it now, she says, "I can't believe I thought I was so fat and disgusting!" When she'd look in the mirror, she hated what she saw.

My mom was raised with the belief that she was not lovable, not enough. From my grandmother's perspective, she was raising my mom to have a nice husband and home life. "I never had to worry about your mothah, because she always got good grades and stayed outta trouble," my grandma told me. Because my mom never got into trouble, she was basically left alone, which meant she never received any positive feedback or reinforcement from her parents. They had five kids. They said to themselves, "Oh good, Janice is fine—we don't need to worry about her." In reality that meant that no matter how much my mom achieved to win their approval, it went unnoticed. My mom continues to struggle with trying to please others and never feels like she does.

While my grandmother did not intentionally raise my mom to feel unlovable, that was the result. Many times parents hurt their children's feelings, self-esteem, and overall sense of value because of their own personal programming that is not related to their children at all. The negative effects are profound and everlasting, until we consciously work to change them.

The Big, the Bad, and the Inadequate

When I was just a toddler, my mom started to become aware that my family members were making negative comments about my size. They would say things like, "Katie is so *big*." My mom recognized that those comments, like the ones she received from her family her whole life, were extremely harmful. She made a strict rule that no one was allowed to use the word *big* when referring to me. My family would also say I was "bad," as my sandy-sweatpants story revealed, because I would not always comply with whatever it was they told me to do.

My mom realized that being raised near our family was going to be a negative experience for me and for her as a parent. She told me once, "When you have kids, everything changes. What you would have accepted for yourself, you won't accept for your children." While this isn't always the case (many times people repeat with their children what they experienced in their own upbringings), this is how my mom felt. We moved away, and my mom did everything she could so that I wouldn't feel the same way she had growing up. I saw our family only once or twice a year. Even then, I understood that I was not well liked.

My grandmother wasn't the only one who gave me messages that I wasn't good enough, which contributed to the self-loathing I felt for so much of my life. Another potent memory dates back to when I was around 12 and had to visit my father in Phoenix, Arizona. I didn't grow up with my dad in my life, and there were two times per year that my brother and I had to go visit him. Essentially, we'd sit on the couch watching TV alone in his apartment all day while he worked. Then when he would get home, we would watch more TV. Out of boredom, I would find myself getting into misadventures, like the time I saw a commercial on TV about trimming bushy eyebrows.

I had huge caterpillar eyebrows and thought maybe I should trim them up a bit. So I grabbed the kitchen scissors and tried to just do a little trim like I had seen on TV. Well, it didn't work out as I planned, and I ended up clipping off half of one eyebrow. I freaked out and immediately called home. Crying and upset, I said, "Ma-ma-moooom . . . I cu-cu-cut off ma-ma-my eyebrow!" I can only imagine what she was thinking. She told me to go find an eyebrow pencil in my stepmom's makeup bag and color it in.

I was feeling pretty good about that idea until I realized that my stepmom didn't have an eyebrow pencil! I was completely embarrassed, and I already felt really judged because my dad would make comments about my brother's and my weight and what we ate. So I decided the best option would be to use my black Crayola marker to just do a touch-up on my little eyebrow situation. I was feeling pretty good about it, but the first thing my dad said when he got home was, "Why do you have black marker on your face?" #fail

Later that night, my dad and uncle were watching the Miss America pageant on TV, commenting on each contestant and rating how "hot" they were. "Wow, she is perfect. She has the perfect body." I remember the anxiety shooting through me in that moment as if it were yesterday. It felt as though someone had punched me right in the gut. If that woman on TV was what my dad thought was perfect and beautiful, then what was I? I sat there with my potbelly and Crayola-stained eyebrow, feeling totally humiliated. From then on, whenever my dad would say I was beautiful, I couldn't help but think, *Yeah, right.* I saw the way he looked at those women, and when he said *they* were perfect, he meant it.

I know for a fact that my dad and uncle will have no memory of this ever happening. Why would they? This was just another routine night for them of watching TV and talking about girls. They were not even aware of what I would hear, think, or feel, yet the memory is indelibly etched in my mind. Every single one of us has moments like this. Maybe you have 1 or 2 memories, or maybe 100, in which someone else made you aware that you were not enough. You see images of how you are supposed to look, and then you go home and have those same ideas not only confirmed but also reinforced by the people you love the most.

A Note to Parents

As a parent, it is important to understand that if we are not consciously evaluating our own programming as well as the media messaging our children receive daily, the odds of our having a negative effect on our children's self-esteem and sense of value are high.

Take my mother, for example. She did an amazing job removing me from a toxic environment that would have hurt my self-image and self-worth. On the other hand, my mom never took the time to challenge her own programming and negative self-image and self-value. Because of that, I followed her example and developed an unhealthy relationship with food, my body, and my self-image.

My mom would tell me, "You are so beautiful. You don't need to lose weight." But in the next breath, she would refer to herself as fat. My mom was on the diet life cycle, which consisted of getting on a new diet, feeling good for a week or two, and then slowly regressing back to where she started . . . followed by feeling terrible and guilty for not losing weight and not sticking to the diet. Then, soon enough, she would start the next diet and continue the cycle. Even though my mom told me I was beautiful the way I was, because she didn't feel the same way about herself, I picked up her subconscious beliefs.

Now, as an adult, I realize that all people, including my parents, are not perfect. They don't know everything, and sometimes they say and do things that can be hurtful. I understand that they are also figuring out who they are and dealing with their personal programming, just like I am. I realize now that of course you can think that both your chubby daughter and a woman in a pageant are beautiful; one's beauty doesn't take away from the other. But, as a child, I interpreted my dad criticizing the food I ate and admiring women who looked nothing like me to mean that I was ugly, wrong, and not enough. When my parents told me I was beautiful, I believed it was a lie, something they said just because they had to.

Oftentimes, parents of teenagers I've worked with tell me things like, "Thank you so much for what you do. I tell my daughter the same things all the time, but she won't believe me." That's because, while there is nothing like a parent's love and acceptance of their children exactly the way they are, you still have to model true self-love and self-acceptance. Kids know authenticity; they will get the message from your actual beliefs about yourself rather than your feelings about them.

Being a parent isn't easy, and it is impossible to say the right thing to your child every time. But we need to be mindful of the messages we give our children, both verbally and nonverbally. Kids are extremely smart and perceptive. They are always learning and receiving messaging, and you must do your best to keep it authentic, truthful, and healthy. To that end, I learned the following mnemonic device, which provides a quick way to decide if what you are about to say to your child is a positive message:

Before you speak, THINK.
T: Is it true?
H: Is it helpful?
I: Is it inspiring?
N: Is it necessary?
K: Is it kind?

My brother has a 10-month-old baby girl, and while I was visiting him a few weeks ago, he told me all his plans for my niece to play various sports. "What if she doesn't like sports?" I asked him. "Oh, she will," he replied. While he was being lighthearted, parents should be aware of unconsciously imposing our own interests and talents onto our children. We need to encourage their natural interests and let them decide who they want to be.

We need to support our children when they go in a direction that is healthy and positive, even if it is not the direction we would have chosen for them or would have been true for ourselves. If you are able to create an environment for your children that has a foundation of authenticity, love, support, and acceptance, then they will stand a much better chance at navigating the world and rejecting negativity and manipulation. They will be strongly connected to their own true sense of self; they will know that they are whole and of value as they are, not as the world tells them they need to be.

Examining Your Programming

Societal programming is strong and varies from person to person, based on countless variables: gender, generation, location, religious background, education level . . . we could go on and on. As we have seen, programming also occurs on a familial level. You were not in control of the messaging you received at home, the meaning you gave it, or how you responded to it. But you can revisit that programming now, examine it, and begin to undo its negative effects.

The first step is understanding the programming of the family members who influenced you. If you look at your family members and start to analyze their programming, you will better understand why they act the way they do. You don't have to agree with them, but understanding the "why" is very important in the healing process.

As children we retain untold amounts of information. Each piece of that information has been downloaded and stored in the database that is our mind. Everything we have seen, heard, touched, smelled, tasted, and experienced has caused an emotion or thought that we store in our subconscious mind. All the information we retain throughout our lives creates our brain's personal programming, which forms our perspectives, beliefs, and reactions. For example, if you have a stored memory that causes pain, when you see, hear, touch, taste, or feel something that triggers that memory, it can cause you to have a negative emotion. For me, I hate beauty pageants. Although that's for several reasons, I am sure the core of my hatred for pageants comes from the painful experience I shared with you earlier.

Again, we cannot control what experiences we had as children or what our mind stored away as data to become part of our programming. So many of us have internalized countless experiences that led us to believe that we are not enough and we are not worthy of love, but as we mature mentally, emotionally, and spiritually and evolve into the best versions of ourselves, we have an opportunity to take our power back. We don't have to just accept all the programming that our mind is running on; we can start to notice, question, and change it. We can become aware of our thoughts and beliefs and begin to assess each one. Here's an exercise that will get you started with this process.

EXERCISE: EXAMINING YOUR FAMILY PROGRAMMING

To jump-start your self-examination, consider any strong thoughts or feelings you had about yourself in childhood and try to track them to a specific source. The following questions are a helpful start. Record your answers however you like (for example, you can write them in a journal or record them on your phone).

- What do you know about how your parents and other family members grew up? Look for patterns of behavior; what beliefs might be motivating them?

- Think about your own upbringing; can you see how your family's programming might have seeped through into yours?

- Do you remember anything that your parents or other family members said or did that made you feel really bad about yourself? What beliefs are revealed by their negative words and actions?

- Growing up, what goals did your parents seem to have for you? Did these match your own goals for yourself? How did that make you feel at the time? How have these experiences affected you as an adult?

. . .

You have a chance to be the ruler of your own mind, removing any negative and harmful viruses that are affecting your operating system. You can decide what programming stays and what needs to go in order for you to live a healthy life that is based on self-love. The more you examine your thoughts and feelings and question them, the more aware you will be of the programs you have stored and the more power you'll have to change your life for the better. We talk about how to do that next.

■ ■ ■ ■ ■

Chapter 8

Break Your
Negative Life Cycle

When you take a closer look at yourself and your pro-gramming, you start to see a pattern—a common theme. Many things people said to me and about me growing up were negative. The beliefs I developed about myself as a result were negative, and the operating system or program-ming I was running on was very negative. I had thoughts like, *Something good like that would never happen to me.* And, *I will never be [fill in the blank with a positive adjective] like that.* Also, *I can't.* I call this a negative life cycle, and these thoughts were the foundation of my identity. Fortunately, I was able to break the cycle, and remove the pattern of negativity from my life; you can do it, too. In this chapter, I explain how.

The Problem with Negativity

My husband and I were eating lunch at a local restaurant, and we happened to sit next to two women on their lunch break from work. One woman gossiped and complained the whole time about all the other women she worked with. Every single thing she said was negative. My husband and I gave each other the "get me away from this lady" look. Her energy was awful, and she was completely unaware of the effect her negativity was having on the people around her— and on her own experiences in life.

Without her realizing it, this woman's negative thought process was subconsciously choosing—and therefore creating—negative experiences for her. *The same is true for all of us.* Our negative beliefs result in negative experiences. Take a moment to let that sink in. For example, how many women do you know who have dated a person who treated them badly? Why would they do that? Each one chose an abusive partner for herself because, subconsciously, she was running on programming that was negative. Thoughts of not being good enough, worthy enough, pretty enough, or lovable led her right into the arms of a person who would reinforce those beliefs. In this way, our negative life cycle becomes compounded and magnified by not only our own negativity but also by the negativity of those we choose to be around.

You cannot have negative beliefs, intentions, and actions and get a positive result. At this stage in your consciousness and self-examination, you are activating your free will and beginning to discover that you can think for yourself. You are beginning to realize that you have the right to decide for yourself who you are, what you want, and who you wish to become. But first you must develop an exit strategy from your current programming—your negative life cycle. With negativity comes judgment, jealousy, envy, and hatred. We cannot begin to restore our spirits and heal our hearts and bodies if all we do is judge, compare, hate, and self-loathe. We cannot have the positive life we desire without letting go of the negative programs we have downloaded along the way.

I used to get so upset with myself and feel tremendous guilt and shame for letting myself get so unhealthy. Looking back now, I realize just how unfair that was. How could I have possibly been a healthy person without any knowledge of how to accomplish that? How could I be upset with myself for not knowing what I didn't know? As an adult I consciously took responsibility for my health and my life, and I sought out that information and knowledge. If I become unhealthy again, then it is my choosing because I now have the information and tools needed to maintain a healthy body.

If you were never presented with the knowledge and tools needed to live a positive, balanced life, how can you be so quick to judge yourself for your negativity? It is time to let the guilt and shame go. You cannot grow and learn with those emotional weights keeping you down.

Become Aware of Your Negative Programming

Let me ask you this: What would you do if you came home and found your house flooded with water? Let's say you opened the front door and saw that water was covering the kitchen floor and beginning to reach the living room carpet. Would you grab some towels and begin sopping up the water to try to stop the carpet from getting ruined? Get a bucket and start to scoop up the water? Or would you first search for the water source to stop the flow of water and then begin to clean up the damage? It is imperative that we locate our source of negativity so we can shut it off. Only then can we work on ourselves from a place of understanding and love. This source is our negative programming.

The first step in changing anything is becoming aware of it. It is key that you begin to notice your thoughts, self-talk, and the things you say to others. You can no longer allow negative thoughts to play on a loop in your mind. Once you become aware of your thoughts, you can change them.

How many times have you gone shopping and been in the fitting room, trying on clothes, and had a whole conversation with yourself? We all do it! What does that conversation sound like? Is it logical and loving? When you try something on and it doesn't fit, do you think, *Nope, that one isn't going to work*? Or do you think, *Nothing fits me because I am disgusting*? Maybe you think to yourself that you're too fat or too thin, or some body part is too small, too big, or just shaped wrong. If only you were *something different*, then surely the clothes would look great on you. How often do you analyze those conversations you have with yourself? Do you even realize you do this? We have these talks with ourselves all day long. What about when you pass by a giant window and can see your reflection as you walk, what do you normally think to yourself? That self-talk is your programming, and that is what you need to begin to police and change!

The best way to become aware of your inner dialogue is to pay attention to your emotional state and to the sensations that happen in your body. When we are upset, our bodies have a physical reaction that tells us something is wrong. Many of us are not attuned to our bodies enough to hear it, but we can be. Once you become aware of how you are feeling, you will be able to take a step back and find the underlying beliefs.

Remember that you can't control your thoughts all the time; we all have moments of negative self-talk. When that happens, it is important to recognize that thoughts are just thoughts and have no power over you unless you allow them to. Gently acknowledge the thoughts, then let go of them, and forgive yourself for having them.

Challenge the Negativity

We do not have to accept the mean thoughts we have about ourselves. The real you is not the voice in your mind that says, *You are not enough*. The real you is the voice that says, *I love you. You are a beautiful and magnificent soul*. It is the voice that will begin to tell the mean girl who is living in your mind to sit down and shut up.

We have the choice of what we focus on and what we tell ourselves. The universe is made from both light and dark, love and hate, good and evil, positive and negative. It is the yin and yang of our nature and that of the world. Our free will is the mechanism by which we get to choose the side of ourselves we would like to feed and nourish.

The story of the two wolves, often presented as a Native American legend, addresses this inner battle. In the parable, an elder explains to his grandson that a fight goes on inside people. Symbolically this fight is between two wolves. One wolf is good and has positive traits, such as peace, joy, love, kindness, and humility. The other wolf is evil and possesses negative qualities, such as anger, greed, arrogance, guilt, and sorrow. After pondering this information, the boy asks which wolf will win. His grandfather replies, "The one you feed."

Which side of yourself have you been nourishing up until now? Your positive or negative side? Your loving or hateful side? The light and beauty of your spirit or the unenlight-ened, learned programming that is blind to the truth?

My friend Ali shared a story with me that is a great example of recognizing and challenging one's negative self-talk. She was seven years old and wearing her mother's beautiful silk dress for a fancy wedding. When her father saw her, he told her that he could see her stomach sticking out through the dress. Girls like her, he scolded, were not allowed to wear dresses like that. Immediately Ali's feelings of happiness and beauty turned to embarrassment, shame, and sadness.

When I asked her if she would ever say something like that to her daughter (or any child, for that matter), Ali emphatically said, "No, never." I then asked Ali if she recognized what programming the experience instilled in her. She replied, "I learned that I was not beautiful. I learned that I needed to always look at other girls who were skinnier than me as an example of who I needed to be in order for my dad to love me. I learned that I couldn't wear certain types of clothing because I was fat." You can see that so much negative programming came from just one experience!

Looking back, Ali was able to consciously evaluate her experience from her 25-year-old perspective and see that she had done nothing wrong and didn't deserve the shame that had resulted. "My dad has some serious issues," she reflected. "He is really screwed up! I can see that what he said really had nothing to do with me—it had everything to do with him and how he felt about himself." Ali then shared that her dad had always cared more about how the family looked than about the family's well-being. He wanted everyone to be blond and tan, even requiring that Ali use a tanning bed when she was in the sixth grade. He was so concerned with wealth, status, and image that he failed to be a connected, loving husband or parent. (Ali's parents have since divorced.)

"So," I said, returning to our discussion about the shame that had been implanted into Ali's head that day of the wedding, "would you say that the negative programming you retained from your experience as a seven-year-old was true or untrue?" Ali had a lightbulb moment and said, "I know it must seem so obvious, but I have never thought of it like that before. No, it is not true. I can wear whatever I want and don't need to be petite in order to do so. And I do think I am beautiful. I am not what he thinks is beautiful, but I also don't have to agree with his opinion of beauty."

If Ali had recognized the programming that came along with her negative self-talk, she could have challenged her beliefs long ago. As an example, let's say a teenage Ali is shopping for prom and decides to try on a really beautiful silk dress. As she looks at herself, she feels bad and thinks, *Oh no, I am not allowed to wear dresses like that because I am not skinny enough.* Her feelings cause her to check in with herself and logically question that thought. Are only skinny people allowed to wear clothes like this? Why does she think that? By finding the source of this negative thought—her traumatic experience when she was seven—she could then reflect on her experiences and challenge her unconscious beliefs.

Be Vigilant

You have learned that when a negative thought pops into your mind, you should acknowledge it, question it, and trace it back to its source so you can shut it off. If you can do this successfully, the cycle of negativity weakens, and eventually there will be a tipping point where positivity outweighs negativity and becomes the prominent energy and experience in your life. Congratulations, you have broken your negative life cycle!

Your work isn't over, however. It takes conscious effort to keep your thoughts consistently positive. There are times when I find myself falling back into old patterns and have to consciously evaluate my self-talk. "Hey, wait a minute! That was really rude and totally not true."

When you're being self-critical, remember to THINK. Ask yourself: Is it True? Helpful? Inspiring? Necessary? Kind?

These questions will also help us stay vigilant in guarding our minds from accepting new programming. We must not forget the power the media has to manipulate our thoughts and generate beliefs that we then unknowingly adopt as our own. However, it is much easier to manipulate the public when we are unaware that we are being manipulated. Once you become aware of your programming and how you have been conditioned—by the media and your immediate environment alike—to not like yourself or your body, the manipulation is no longer as effective. It's like knowing the secret behind a magic trick.

EXERCISE: LOCATING AND CHANGING A PARTICULAR NEGATIVE BELIEF

This exercise is going to assist you in identifying, locating, and challenging your negative programming. You will examine and evaluate your thoughts and beliefs to decide if they are impostors—having come from or belonging to someone else—that were implanted in your mind to feed a negative life cycle, or if they were created from your authentic, true self. You may want to record your responses in writing, to help solidify your thoughts.

- Recall a time when someone made you aware that you were not good enough. How did you feel? (Remember the feelings Ali described in her story of the dress.)

- Are there similar circumstances in which you continue to experience the same negative feelings? How has that one experience affected you to this day?

- What beliefs did you develop based on that experience? What thoughts have you simply accepted as true without questioning them?

- Now, looking back, do you think that the beliefs you developed about yourself are logical and accurate?

- Even if the beliefs were true, were they also helpful, inspiring, necessary, and kind?

- Does the belief or programming you installed from that experience serve you and honor your true self? Does it strengthen you or does it hurt you?

- What reasons do you have for maintaining this belief? Are there any benefits you can think of?

- Make the decision to change your thoughts— what positive statement can replace your negative belief?

This exercise is a great way of developing the habit of questioning your beliefs before you accept them as true and live your life based on them. As you locate one faucet of negativity and shut it off, you may be led right to the next, then the next, and the next, and so on. That is the goal! If you need to fill up an entire notebook with memories for this exercise, do it. When you begin to challenge your beliefs about yourself, you'll see that hiding painful memories away no longer serves you. Those beliefs, memories, and experiences are the foundation of your negative programming and they are what you are going to identify, locate, and challenge so they can be released.

For example, a woman I worked with told me that she was called "thunder thighs" when she was in junior high school. As a result, she never wore shorts and hated her legs. In examining that belief from her adult perspective, she acknowledged that, yes, she has large, muscular thighs. But then she challenged the belief that said having larger legs was a bad thing. What about having larger legs is objectively bad? Why would having large, strong legs mean that a person shouldn't wear shorts on a hot summer day? She realized that this belief did not come from her, nor did it strengthen her, and she recognized that she was free to change it now. This is the work you are going to do here.

■ ■ ■

A lot of our negative programming, both societal and familial, centers on beauty: what it is, and whether we meet its requirements. As you have no doubt experienced, the beauty ideal that has been programmed into us can bring up negative thoughts and emotions, resulting in the damaging condition of self-loathing. In Chapter 9, we examine and challenge our ingrained beliefs about beauty—so we can ultimately redefine beauty for ourselves.

■ ■ ■ ■ ■

Chapter 9

Redefine Beauty

It should be clear by now that our concept of beauty is heavily influenced from the outside—by society, by the advertising industry, and even by our families. When narrow definitions of physical attractiveness are so ingrained in us, we have no idea what true beauty is. Even companies that try to broaden the representation of beauty with "real beauty" campaigns, as we discussed in Chapter 3, are still defining beauty for us. So what does true beauty even mean?

The bottom line is that we do not need companies to tell us what beauty is—nor can we count on them to represent our version of beauty. I am sure there are millions of women just like me searching for where they fit. We all want to be part of a group where we can rejoice and celebrate who we are. Instead of looking for a brand image that we can fit into, we need to redefine beauty as something unique to each of us.

Beauty Ideals around the World

Perhaps the most convincing argument for challenging the Western beauty ideal is to remember that beauty ideals differ from culture to culture—which is to say, *there is no single definition of beauty.* Learning about what is considered beautiful in other parts of the world was a huge eye-opener for me. By sharing some of these global concepts of beauty, I hope to give you the same transformative experience I had. Challenging the idea of a single ideal is a preliminary step in forming your *own* definition of beauty. One note I'd like to make is that, historically, cultures in different parts of the world possessed beauty ideals that were distinct and unique to each heritage. But today, because Western media is now accessible around the world, local perceptions of beauty are blending and changing.

— *Tiny Feet:* For centuries, a three- or four-inch foot was considered the height of beauty for Chinese women. In fact, girls who did not participate in "foot binding" were considered unmarriageable. To achieve this, the toes of a very young girl were broken and pushed back against the sole of the foot, then tightly bound with bandages. The foot was continuously broken and wrapped over the next couple of years to keep them tiny and hooflike. To compensate, women with bound feet developed leg muscles and a unique way of walking, which were viewed as erotic by men. This incredibly painful practice was thought to represent cultural identity, beauty, and moral feminine behavior. Thankfully the practice of foot binding was banned in 1912, but the male-dominated society in China is still a strong reality.

— *Beautiful Fat:* In the African country of Mauritania, being thin is traditionally viewed as unattractive, while larger girls are deemed to be of higher class, status, and beauty. To provide their daughters with better opportunities for marriage, some families will forcibly fatten their young girls in a practice known as *leblouh.* There are even "fat farms" that will force-feed fattening foods to girls to help them pack on the pounds. This beauty tradition has moved in and out of favor with the times, and was even outlawed for a while; about 20 percent of women participated in leblouh in 2008.

— *Long Necks:* On the border between Thailand and Myanmar, the Kayan tribe has a beauty ideal that is entirely unique. When Kayan girls are five years old, they have brass coils wrapped around their necks, the weight of which pushes down the muscles around their collarbones to give the illusion of a long neck covered by golden rings. They continue to add coils every year, and a full set of coils can weigh over 20 pounds, although few women wear a full set. There are many myths surrounding the origin of these neck rings, but today they are considered a form of body decoration and a way to preserve cultural identity.

It is clear that the word *beauty* has many different meanings and symbols in our world. The symbols of beauty in Western culture have caused us to have many negative thoughts and emotions connected with the idea of beauty. I am going to ask you again to throw that programming away, to wipe the slate clean, so that you can properly use your free will to evaluate beauty from a nonbiased place. To understand the vast entity that is beauty, we need to break down our beliefs about it first.

Keeping It Real

For our own physical and mental well-being, it is necessary to give beauty our own meaning, based on very personal criteria. I can't tell you what real beauty is because it is different for each person. And discovering that for yourself is what this book is all about! You now have the opportunity to define what beauty means to *you*.

The *Oxford Dictionary* definition of *beauty* is "a combination of qualities, such as shape, color, or form, that please the aesthetic senses, especially the sight." You'll note that there is no single physical description of what is beautiful. So, according to this definition, beauty is just something that is pleasing to the senses. As you construct your own personal definition of beauty, I want you to keep this in mind. True, real, or authentic beauty is pleasing to your senses—but not only your senses. It is also pleasing to your heart. It uplifts your spirit, and makes you feel happy—even joyous.

Sometimes beauty can't be perceived by the senses at all; it comes from within. For example, you might find a genuine smile or a sparkle in the eye to be beautiful. You might perceive confidence and courage to be incredibly alluring. Perhaps you think being kind to others is the most stunning feature a person can possess. Maybe a great sense of humor is the sexiest thing ever. Or perhaps you see *everyone* as beautiful, because you are able to look past a person's surface attributes and psychological programming to his or her inherent perfection.

You might be surprised by how your definition of beauty changes as you begin to focus less on the image of beauty you have been sold and more on the *experience* of beauty you have been denying. When we are conditioned to perceive beauty as a limited view of the female body, we are desensitized and blinded to the beauty that is all around and within us. We unknowingly give away our right to actively experience beauty and receive the positivity it brings to the world and to our lives.

I feel fortunate to have the opportunity to work in the fashion industry as a model; as the owner of a modeling agency; and as a role model when I educate high school students about media manipulation, body image, and self-love. My multiple roles allow me to keep a healthy perspective on beauty and reject the media's view of "normal."

For instance, the fashion and entertainment industries sell a false image of teenage girls to the public. It is an image that is manipulated to look flawless, seductive, and mature rather than young, bright-eyed, happy, and a little awkward. When I go into a high school and look around, what I see is *real.* I see every body type, size, shape, color, and height. I am quickly reminded that teenage girls do not look like models— yet they are so naturally beautiful. They have a happy, innocent glow about them. They look so much younger than the media's depictions of the "sexy teenager." These girls have little round faces, and some of them have braces and glasses. They love wearing hoodies, jeans, and messy buns rather than the high-fashion looks sold in magazines. Recognizing what's *really* real is the first step toward defining beauty for ourselves.

I want you to remember another point: beauty is always positive. If you come across something or someone who embodies and causes negativity, yet whom the world perceives as beautiful, take note. This is a false representation of beauty. Authentic beauty cannot cultivate and embody the negative. We must choose for ourselves which kind of beauty we would like to represent and embody: the kind that causes self-harm and negativity and leaves us feeling unfulfilled, or the kind that fills our souls and inspires goodness, kindness, hope, love, and all things positive.

EXERCISE: DEFINING BEAUTY FOR YOURSELF

Challenge the programming you've received about beauty by assessing what you experience as beautiful in one day. Now, if you interpret that as "people watching" and casting judgment on the looks of passersby, you are missing the point. That is not what I want you to do at all. Instead, without holding judgment for others or yourself, evaluate your interactions with others and your environment based on the three basic qualities of beauty presented in this chapter:

- Beauty is pleasing to the senses.
- Beauty is pleasing to the heart.
- Beauty is positive.

Notice the things and people who meet these criteria for you. While a thing or person may be pleasing to the senses, the heart, or both, beauty *must* be associated with positivity—no negativity allowed. The main indicator of what you find beautiful is how you *feel*: uplifted, delighted, or even elated.

For example, perhaps you get up early enough to witness a particularly vibrant sunrise. The gold, crimson, and purple hues spreading across the sky are pleasing to your sight; the pure majesty of the heavens reminds you of your oneness with the universe; and the experience feels very positive overall.

Applying the criteria to people you know or to strangers, you might observe such examples of beauty as adorable freckles on a girl's cheeks, a whimsical hat worn by a senior citizen, the sweet voice of a woman talking to her infant, witty banter with a barista at the coffee shop, an inspiring news story about someone's selfless act, having the elevator held for you, and so on.

Conscious Beauty

On your journey to discover what beauty means to you, always ask yourself, "Is this kind of beauty serving my true self?" In other words, is this idea of beauty a positive or negative addition to your sense of self? Keep the forms of beauty you discover along the way that are positive and push you forward; toss aside the ones that are being sold to you with a hidden agenda whereby someone else benefits by keeping you small.

Having said that, it's important to realize that beauty itself is not the enemy! Rather, it is our narrow definition of beauty that needs to change. As you begin to consciously create who you are, you will recognize that it is your right to challenge society's definition of beauty. After all, you do not have to accept the vision of beauty that would require you to coil brass in rings around your neck. You do not need to bleach your skin, or force-feed yourself, or bind your feet. And you do not need to deny your body of the nourishment it needs while feeding your mind negative thoughts, leaving your soul starving for purpose, in order to be beautiful and pleasing to others in the tradition of the Western beauty ideal.

You are a human being. You are a soul or spirit that has been given a body to experience this physical life. You have the right to create a definition of beauty for yourself that is based on what is true for you. The only limitations beauty possesses are the ones you place on it and the ones you accept for yourself.

■ ■ ■

To believe that you are not beautiful is in a sense denying your very essence here on earth. Every single person is a beautiful and real being deserving of love. You could never be defined by something as limiting as your body or your face. We're always beautiful when we're coming from our spirit—the nurturing, compassionate, and loving energy we all share. It is impossible *not* to be beautiful when we're coming from that place. Speaking of energy, in Chapter 10 we examine just what this powerful force is and how it relates to your experience of life.

■ ■ ■ ■ ■

Chapter 10

Harness the Power of Your Thoughts

Is attaining wellness truly simple? According to Dr. Richard Schulze, it can be: "All you have to do is *stop* doing what is making you sick, and *start* living new and healthy ways that will heal you." I have found this logical and intuitive philosophy to be unquestionably true as well as applicable to life itself. By letting go of a negative life cycle, you get rid of all things that are unhealthy for you physically, mentally, emotionally, and spiritually—and your life begins to heal. By removing the influences that are harming you, you create space for what is positive and nourishing to enter. By doing so, you honor and cultivate your inner greatness.

When you choose to shift from negative to positive, from self-loathing to self-love, you will find that the energy of your body, your thoughts, and the rest of your being changes—and this, amazingly, will affect your whole world.

Your life will, almost miraculously, begin to look and feel better. "How?" you ask. It all goes back to that thing I just mentioned—energy. In this chapter, we talk about energy as the scientific basis of reality. We then look at one incredibly powerful form of energy—thought energy. Our thoughts can have a tremendous impact on our lives, for better or worse.

Everything Is Energy

All physical reality is made up of energy! The great theoretical physicist Albert Einstein said: "Mass and energy are both but different manifestations of the same thing." Indeed, quantum physics reveals that *thought*, as well as matter, is vibrational. You, just as you are now, are vibrating at your own unique frequency. Take a moment to really think about that!

Additionally, there is a phenomenon called "sympathetic vibration," in which a body vibrates when a nearby body with the same basic frequency vibrates. For example, if you have two similar tuning forks, when one fork is struck and moved close to the other, the unstruck fork will start to vibrate. Our energy also acts like that—having an effect on others who come into our space.

Have you ever walked into a room and known that something intense has just gone down? You feel it. The energetic vibration in the room is affecting your own vibration. We pick up on the energy of the people we surround ourselves with, and we also have the ability to affect others through our energy. Looked at this way, we can say that energy is either positive or negative, constructive or destructive, life promoting or life decreasing. This is why you need to surround yourself with kind, positive, and loving people if that is the energy you want to experience. Likewise, we need to influence others positively by having good energy ourselves.

Oprah Winfrey once shared that for years she had a sign hanging in her makeup room that said: PLEASE TAKE RESPONSIBILITY FOR THE ENERGY YOU BRING INTO THIS SPACE. She affirmed, "We are all beaming little signals like radio frequencies, and the world is responding in kind." Oftentimes we don't even recognize the energy we send out. When there are a lot of people in one space, our vibrations and energy are affected by others unless we become aware and consciously protect ourselves and remember that ultimately our energy is our choice.

I recently experienced a great example of this. I was on a flight from New York to Los Angeles, and I had a window seat way in the back of the plane. The five-year-old boy in the seat in front of me was extremely loud; he was traveling with his grandmother, who you could tell had no idea how to handle him. Less than five minutes after I sat down, the man seated in front of this boy had already turned around and forcefully told him to stop kicking his seat. With the grandmother feeling overwhelmed, the boy being unsettled and loud, and the nearby passengers growing angry, I found myself and my energy starting to feel negative. Instead of allowing that to happen, I leaned my head against the window and began to think about how I might take my power over my mood back.

The little boy also leaned his head against the window and looked back at me. "Hi. What's your name?" I asked him.

"Hi. Kyle," he said. He looked shocked that I spoke to him in a normal, conversational tone. "What are you doing back there?"

"I am getting ready to take off. What are you doing up there?" I asked.

"Are we going to go up in the clouds?" he asked as he pointed to the sky.

"Yes, we are, but the sun is going to go down and people are going to be sleeping, so we have to be a little quieter." I lowered my voice, and he too began to speak more softly.

"I am going to see my mom and her boyfriend," he said.

"Wow, that sounds like so much fun. I am sure she can't wait to see you," I replied.

We continued our conversation with our heads against the windows, looking at each other through the crack between our seats. Then it was time for takeoff.

Distracted by our conversation and the anticipation of takeoff, Kyle had calmed down. He had a few more outbursts, but when he would look back at me, I would remind him that people were going to sleep. He'd nod in understanding and put his finger up to his lips and make the "shhhhh" sound.

Everything was great for about 10 minutes until Kyle had a total meltdown—complete with screaming and kicking. His grandmother sat silent, not saying a word or attempting to assist him. The man in front of Kyle turned around and yelled at him again, only fueling the situation. Across the aisle in my row was a mother traveling with her two children. She immediately tried to help, offering Kyle snacks and some water. No one knew what to do, and everyone was becoming frustrated and sending negative vibes toward Kyle.

At that point I instinctively stood up, leaned over the top of his seat, and said, "Hi, Kyle," in a calm, normal voice. "I can tell you are uncomfortable. I have an extra set of headphones. Would you like me to put on some cartoons for you to watch?"

He stopped screaming and crying. He looked up at me, surprised, and said, "Yeah."

"Okay, but I need your help. Can you help me plug in the cord?" Kyle assisted me, and within 20 minutes he was asleep. We didn't hear another sound from him the entire flight!

Now, I could have handled that situation in many ways. I could have rolled my eyes, breathed heavily, and allowed my attitude and energy to be affected by those around me. Or I could have chosen, as I did, to use good energy to help improve the situation. By connecting with Kyle, letting him know that I understood he was uncomfortable and that he needed help, and then offering my help, he was able to receive the comfort he had been looking for.

EXERCISE: NOTICING ENERGY

Spend a day noticing the energy of others around you. All day, I want you to choose a person near you and assess what kind of energy he or she is putting off. Remember to not base this assessment on the superficiality of looks, because, as the saying goes, looks really can be deceiving. You can use the following list of words as a starting point:

- Positive

- Happy

- Pleasant

- Generous

- Fun

- Flirty

- Kind

- Loving

- Playful

- Sweet

- Negative

- Moody

- Sad

- Tired

- Bored

- Angry

- Grumpy

- Pushy

- Frustrated

- Entitled

Once you've felt the "experience" of this person, end your evaluation by categorizing the person's energy as being positive or negative, healthy or unhealthy, for you. Then choose another person, and notice his or her energy.

The Power of Your Thoughts

So far we have seen that all matter in the physical world is energy, or vibration. We have also touched on the idea that thoughts are energy, and our thoughts can have a powerful effect on what happens in our lives. According to William Walker Atkinson, a pioneer of the New Thought movement, "Thought is a force—a manifestation of energy—having a magnet-like power of attraction." If you have a positive out-look, you see people and experiences as safe and exciting. If you come from a negative point of view, you could see the same people and experiences as dangerous and to be feared.

Energy, especially thought energy, may in fact be one of the most powerful things any of us possesses. When you realize that the energy you put out is what you will in turn attract, you can begin to consciously evaluate your thoughts and the outcomes they produce in your life. John Assaraf, a brain researcher and CEO of NeuroGym, explains this brilliantly:

> You literally become what you think about most. Your life becomes what you have imagined and believed in most. The world is literally your mirror, enabling you to experience in the physical plane what you hold as your truth . . . until you change it.
>
> Quantum physics shows us that the world is not the hard and unchangeable thing it may appear to be. Instead, it is a very fluid place continuously built up using our individual and collective thoughts. What we think is true is really an illusion, almost like a magic trick. Fortunately, we have begun to uncover the illusion and, most importantly, how to change it. . . .
>
> What is your body made of? . . . What are tissues and organs made of? Cells. What are cells made of? Molecules. What are molecules made of? Atoms. What are atoms made of? Subatomic particles. What are subatomic particles made of? Energy!
>
> You and I are pure energy-light in its most beautiful and intelligent configuration. Energy that is constantly changing beneath the surface, and you control it all with your powerful mind.
>
> You are one big stellar and powerful Human Being.

Our reality serves as a mirror to our thoughts and beliefs. Your life as it is now is a direct reflection of how you think and feel about yourself. Up until now, you may not have realized the power the media has had over your thoughts, self-image, and desires. You may not have understood how society has taught you to abandon your authentic self in favor of conforming to a more acceptable version that others will feel safe with and approve of. There is a lot going on here, and it is important to not get overwhelmed. Take a deep breath and realize that you picked up this book for a reason. Once you understand how your life has reached its current state, you can change your thoughts and move forward to create a life that is everything you desire it to be.

As a teenager, after I had grown out of my chubby stage and into my five-nine frame, I weighed 150 pounds. Although I was at a healthy weight, I hated my body and told myself I was fat for so long. Then, during my freshman year of college, my body became a reflection of my perception and beliefs. After gaining weight, I would work out because I was disgusted with myself. When I looked in the mirror, I felt shame, embarrassment, and guilt. Even though my real image in the world was not that overweight, the image I had of myself was.

The thoughts I had about myself were awful—completely negative. As a result of not appreciating, loving, and valuing my body, and having nothing but negative thoughts about it, over time my body became more and more what I had thought all along. I would eat unhealthy foods in an effort to feel better in the moment. I did not move my body or exercise as an act of self-love; I just looked in the mirror and thought awful things about myself.

Open Yourself Up to More Possibilities

One thing that limits many of us from being open to a more positive reality is the fear of rejection. For example, you might see a cute person and think, "I'd love to go out with him/her, but I'm too fat/ugly/shy/weird for him/her." What you have done is limited your opportunities by deciding what someone else will think based on your own insecurities. The other person has nothing to do with it! Your own negative thoughts limited that possibility. He or she never got a chance to decide, yet you blame him or her for your own self-limiting behavior.

When you notice yourself engaging in limiting self-talk, examine the belief more closely. What's the worst that could happen if you go for it anyway? If you ask someone out and he or she says, "No thanks," absolutely nothing has changed. That wasn't the right person for you, otherwise he or she would have seen your greatness. Furthermore, the response you get might be totally unrelated to you.

The fear of rejection should not rule your life. So what if everyone doesn't love you? Only *you* have to love you. I'm sure you have turned down someone without giving it a thought. My husband sums this up with a great analogy: There are 31 flavors for a reason. Everyone likes something different. Even that funky, weird flavor in the back has a scoop out of it because it is *someone's* favorite.

Seeing the Power of Thoughts

When I started to teach about the power of thought in schools, my favorite example to use to illustrate the concept was Dr. Masaru Emoto's famous water experiments. Dr. Emoto performed a series of experiments observing the physical effects of words, pictures, music, and prayer on the crystalline structure of water. He used microscopic photography to capture images of water molecules after they had been exposed to different variables and then frozen.

The frozen water exposed to positive thoughts, when viewed under a microscope, had crystals that appeared perfectly symmetrical and aesthetically pleasing. They were white and beautiful, rather like a snowflake. The crystals in the frozen "negative thought" water resembled bubbling brown tar. Dr. Emoto provided tangible evidence that our thoughts, both negative and positive, have the power to affect the structure of water. If thoughts can have that effect on water, then what can they do to us, since human beings are approximately 60 percent water?

EXERCISE: REPLACING NEGATIVITY WITH POSITIVE THOUGHTS

If you were frozen right now, what would the crystalline structure of your molecules—based on your thinking—look like? Start recognizing your limiting self-talk, and then consciously replace it with ideas that encourage what you want to experience and create.

From this point on, become aware of your thoughts and rid yourself of negativity by doing the following:

- Consciously pay attention to your feelings and thoughts. (Remember, one sign that you are thinking negatively is having feelings of upset.)

- When you notice yourself having a negative thought or engaging in an unproductive habit, acknowledge it. What are you fearful of? Rejection? Embarrassment? Not being good enough? Simply identifying this feeling will be helpful.

- Examine the source or "faucet" of negativity, so that you can shut it off. Where in your past did this fear or belief or habit come from? Is it really yours, or did it originally come from someone or somewhere else?

- Change the negative thought by replacing it with a positive one. Putting the positive out there will bring what you are looking for to you. If, for example, it is the fear of rejection, stop the talk in your head that says, "He is never going to like me," and replace it with, "Anyone would be lucky to spend time with me," or "I am fun, relaxed, and basically *awesome*," or "My higher power has a plan for me, and he might be lucky enough to be part of it." Do you see the difference?

Repeat these steps as many times as you need to. The goal is to replace all your negative thoughts and just watch how your life changes! I really encourage you to continue to think about your life positively and expect it to be awesome.

By following these steps, you will begin to realize how often negative thoughts sabotage your healthy and positive efforts. You can then choose to no longer accept that for yourself, and work to correct the problem. Because we have so many negative thoughts, this is not an overnight fix. But as you become more empowered and aware of who you are, you will become even more aware of who you are *not* and more easily let those negative things go!

■ ■ ■

The tools I provided in this chapter will help you stay on track, operating on self-love and positivity, and radiating positive and loving energy into the world—which will enable you to attract the like in return. Now, that is beautiful! In Chapter 11, we look specifically at the connection between thoughts and the body.

■ ■ ■ ■ ■

Chapter 11

Change Your Mind about Your Body

Multiple times in this book I have asked you to start over. I asked you to wipe your mind clean of the media and societal programming that disconnected you from your true self. That involved taking a closer look at several different aspects of your life, such as your self-image, your family, your belief system, and the beauty ideal, to name a few. I have asked you to start over and develop a new way of thinking that is more positive, loving, and nurturing. Now I am going to ask you to start over once again. This time I want you to forgive yourself for your past judgments on, and your unhealthy relationship with, your body. It is time to start anew.

Before we get started, I would like you to think of your favorite photo of yourself as a child. We all have one. Mine captures the time I decided to cut my own hair in the bathroom at four years old. My mom snapped a picture of me smiling with my crazy hair and my little belly hanging out, which I thought looked awesome! When you have a chance, I want you to find that photo; then, keep it close, where you can look at it frequently.

As you begin to change your thoughts, you will see your life begin to change as a result. This shift can cause you to feel a little shaky and doubt yourself. That image of you as a child will serve as a reminder that even when the world seems chaotic and you question who you are, you know your truth. She will be right there staring back at you, reminding you that you are always deserving of love, happiness, and all things good.

Simple but Not Easy

Accepting your body as it is and changing your thoughts to be positive is not necessarily easy, because programming and habits are by definition ingrained. But with enough clarity and desire, it is totally possible.

I would like you to look back over the years at the ups and downs with your body and make peace with the old relationship you had with it. Learn from your experiences, forgive yourself for your mistakes, and let it all go, so that you can begin to build the relationship with your body that you both deserve. It is time to create a lasting, loving relationship with your body, not just a one-night stand of fleeting positive feelings.

This new relationship is going to be built on friendship, understanding, compassion, and love. The relationship you build with your body is the ultimate example of positive intention, commitment, and trust. Your body is your vessel in which you experience this world. In moving forward in your new relationship with your body, it is imperative to remember that you are not *just* a body and to start to value your experiences in this life and your glorious existence above all else. This starts with acceptance of your body exactly as it is today. The next exercise will help you do that.

EXERCISE: MAKING FRIENDS WITH YOUR BODY

The term *mind-body-spirit* represents the three aspects of the self. Your body is a vessel for your mind and your spirit, or soul. Basically, your body is a vehicle for your consciousness to experience this earthly life with. Despite being made up of mind-body-spirit, most of the time we focus only on the body. Yet the greater the connection between these three aspects of self, the more whole and present and "ourselves" we feel. To connect them, we need to get them talking to each other. The following letter-writing exercise will help you do so.

- Write a letter to your body. Really take a moment, think about your relationship with your body so far in your life, and then begin writing your letter, starting with "Dear Body."

- Just relax and let whatever comes flow. Write whatever you feel; there is no right or wrong here. You will be surprised at what surfaces.

- When you are done, take a moment to read the letter and examine what came up that you weren't previously aware of. What feelings did you experience while writing this letter to your body? What emotions surfaced afterward?

- Next, I want you to have your body write back! (Even if this sounds a little silly, what have you got to lose?) There are no wrong answers; just let it flow.

- Read the letter and think about the feelings and memories that surface.

Your Body Wants to Be Heard

I did the exercise of making friends with your body with the participants of one of my body-image workshops, and the outcome was amazing. People were able to share their letters with the group if they wanted to, and every person's letter was so different and beautiful in its own way. What many people realize from this exercise is that they have never taken the time to communicate with themselves fully.

Have you ever stopped to truly listen to the needs and wants of your body? Until now you have been mainly operating on the wants of your mind, the same "wants" that were put there by the media to manipulate you into buying more products or that were put there by people in your life to get you to conform so they could feel safe or comfortable around you.

You didn't buy those diet pills or "skinny tea" because your body was talking to you and saying, "Hey, self, you know, I have been thinking, I would love to have some random heart palpitations and feel like I am on the verge of a heart attack at any given moment. Oh, and if you could also get me some of that tea that will make me shit my pants in public, that would be *a-mazing*." No, of course not! Your body—which is designed to be healthy and is always working to repair and heal itself—would never choose to put harmful substances in its system, starve itself, or eat so unhealthily that it lowers your quality of life. Your body is an incredible feat of nature and the universe and nothing short of a miraculous gift.

When I look back at my old relationship with my body, I think of my body as that superkind and sweet person we all know who is so eager to please and, because of that, gets taken advantage of. My body was easy to blame for my actions because it couldn't talk back! I couldn't believe I had been such a bully to my own body, who was the innocent party in the war I waged against it. My body played no role in my eating unhealthy foods, my thinking negative thoughts, or my choosing to sit on the couch versus going outside to do something physical. *I* chose that for my body and then took no responsibility for *my* actions. Instead I just blamed my body for not looking how it was "supposed" to look according to what society said was beautiful. Now, is that fair?

Does any of this sound familiar? While the details might change from person to person, the underlying theme remains the same. We all are guilty of making choices based on our mind's wants versus actually listening to and caring for the needs of our body. We all are guilty of living a negative life cycle that consists of negative thoughts about our body that result in negative actions and habits that result in negatively reinforcing experiences in our life—ultimately leaving us feeling disconnected from our body altogether. We—mind, body, *and* soul—deserve so much better!

Your Body Loves You—Start Loving It Back!

From the beginning your body has loved you, every day of your life. Your respiratory system has brought in life-sustaining oxygen. Your heart has pumped blood to your tissues and organs. Your immune system has fought against infection and illness. Your body has been with you and has shared both your favorite experiences in life and also the ones that were traumatic and caused you harm.

In every experience you've had, you were not alone; as people come and go in your life, your body is always there. Your body is there when you decide to sit on the couch and do nothing, and it is there when you decide to push it to the extremes of activity. Your body is the vessel that your mind and your soul have been given to experience this life. When you look at your body from this perspective, you might ask yourself, "What did my body ever do to me to make me hate it so much?" It is time to stop condemning this aspect of yourself that gives you the very ability to live in this world!

Our relationships with our bodies start out healthy and happy as children. We enjoy it, exercise it, and feel totally comfortable in it. It's kind of like with our first love—we expect it to be this way forever. Then we are unconsciously and consciously exposed to unrealistic expectations and judgments of our body by society, media, and other people. As we grow, we start to infuse negativity into the relationship by not appreciating our body, wishing it were different, and treating it badly. This creates a separation between our body and our mind and soul that leaves a space for self-deprivation and negativity to take hold.

The unrealistic skinny beauty ideal we are expected to aspire to is literally fostering a culture of malnourished females. Some girls and women restrict their food intake and skip meals in the fear of getting fat; others are stuck on the yo-yo diet cycle, repeatedly losing and gaining weight. I have yet to meet a woman who has not had an unhealthy relationship with food at *some* point. And when we deny ourselves proper nutrition, we unknowingly inhibit our own brain function! A malnourished body and a foggy brain cannot make a strong mind-body-spirit connection.

By writing a letter to my body and then writing a response from my body to me, I realized that my body, mind, and soul all have different needs. Looking at my body as the amazing, loving, innocent, and accommodating entity that it is, I felt horrible for the way I had treated it. My body did not deserve the years of punishment I had put it through. By understanding that my body has unconditional love for me—and is there to help me have a meaningful life—I was able to make peace with it. It became clear to me that I need to love and honor my body for the miraculous vehicle that it is. It is the vehicle that was designed specifically for me and will continue to carry me as faithfully through this life as I enable it to. The first step to loving my body was putting a stop to judging it negatively.

What You See in the Mirror

Before coming to the realization that my body deserves admiration for all the amazing things and experiences it provides me on a daily basis, I was in a low place. At my largest size, I remember looking in the mirror before getting in the shower and thinking, *Who* is *that person?* I felt trapped in someone else's body. I looked at my rolls and love handles with disgust, wishing for them to disappear. Yet when I was at my smallest size, I found myself looking in the mirror and thinking, *Ew, now my boobs look like empty raisin sacks and my hips are still not small enough.* One problem I needed to "fix" quickly morphed into another, leaving me in a downward spiral of perfectionism.

When you look in the mirror and think horrible things about your body, what kind of beauty do you possess in that moment? The thoughts I had and the energy I allowed to pass through me were not beautiful at all. They were negative, mean, and just plain ugly. If you rationally think about what I am saying here, I hope you can ask yourself, "Is my body really ugly, gross, unattractive, and repulsive? Or is it my energy and thoughts that are?"

You Are Not Just Your Body

We believe that if we are skinny and fit the beauty ideal, we will have greater value. Maybe there is truth to that—at least, we may be more *valued*. There are people who will treat you better if you look the way they want you to. You could receive more attention from others, date more people, have more followers on social media, and even possibly have more opportunities. At the end of the day, however, it won't be meaningful. It will feel like being used. To fit the ideal that our society has created for women to be of value, you must choose pleasing others over pleasing yourself. What this kind of thinking *can* guarantee is that you will live your life seeking acceptance from others based on only one small aspect of the real you—your body.

Your body does not represent who you are as a spirit or being. That being said, it can be a living expression of the real you if you allow it to be. Your soul is a unique energy of its own, which also emanates out into the world. When you use your mind to pass judgment on your body, you are creating a split between your essence (the soul) and it (the body). In effect, you are denying your soul its vessel.

Every time you think hateful thoughts toward your body, you are in fact reinforcing the belief that you are not worthy of your experience here on earth. Every time you look at another woman's body and think, *I wish I looked like her*, or you comment "#bodygoals" on an Instagram image, you are really saying, "I am not enough." By looking at yourself through nonjudgmental eyes, however, you can see that your vessel is perfectly worthy, and its well-being is in your hands.

Choosing Your True Self, Once and for All

And that's where you find yourself today. You have reached a pivotal point on your path to self-love where you must choose one of two options. Option one is to accept that you are "lesser than." Your role in this life is to please others with your physical body, which must look how others decide it should look and do what others decide it should do.

Option two is to stop conforming to a society that does not honor the goodness that you already are. Instead of abandoning your soul, choose to detach from society and its negative view of who you are and who you are allowed to be. Own your rightful space in this world as the unique, handcrafted work of art that you truly are. We can choose to recognize that we are more than a body—we are a beautiful combination of a physical body; an open and intentional mind; and a kind, loving soul. That is what we must see when we look in the mirror.

For many years, I lived in limbo. I wasn't fully committed to option one, but I did see myself as just a physical body and placed my value there. Yet I still struggled internally with fully accepting that belief. I knew I was missing something, and it is only now that I realize that all the things I put my body and mind through were my attempts to fill that void. I pursued what others believed was valuable: signing with the top modeling agencies in the world, being a *Sports Illustrated* swimsuit model, working nonstop as a model, and wearing the crown of success that all those things promised me. Still, I was failing, not because of my body but because I was searching for my meaning and value in the wrong places.

Everyone has had a moment when she wanted to just give up on herself. In each of those moments, there was something within me that said, "Keep going." When I started listening to that part of me, I realized that it was my soul talking! That was my true self fighting for me and helping me understand why I am here. All the times I felt lost or alone, I wasn't. I had my body there with me, loving me unconditionally, and I had my soul guiding me and whispering, "Don't give up," when I needed it most. My body was never the problem; my mind was what needed to change.

That's what I'm here to help you do—change the unhealthy way your thinking is harming you on every level of your being and preventing you from having the glorious life you deserve. In the next exercise, we put this idea into practice. It will take a bit of courage, but I know you can succeed. Okay, let's do this!

EXERCISE: LOOKING IN THE MIRROR: WHAT DO YOU CHOOSE TO SEE?

We have all looked in the mirror naked and thought awful things about our bodies and critiqued every perceived flaw. Now I'd like you to step again in front of the mirror, only this time I want you to look at your naked body and see it for what it *actually* is—a miraculous and beautifully designed vehicle that you have been given in order to experience this life.

Yes, you read that right—this exercise is to look at yourself naked in the mirror!

I want you to know that I understand how hard this idea might be at first. I realize that looking at your naked body in the mirror is an extremely brave thing to do! It can evoke a lot of negative thoughts and emotions like shame, fear, self-hatred, sadness, and disgust.

The goal is to look at your body without judgment or fear—to evaluate your body for what it *truly* is and not for how it compares with what the media has made you believe it should be.

So before you look at your reflection, I want you to take it all off . . . take off your judgments, negativity, shame, comparisons, self-loathing, and fear. Only after doing so should you take off whatever clothing you have on.

Look at your body. Examine the beautiful vehicle that is going to be your faithful partner to the end. *Feel* your beauty; become aware of your energy. Remember that your body is actually your greatest ally and most loyal friend.

Tending to Your True Self

Acceptance, love, friendship, and appreciation are the foundation of your new relationship with your body. No matter how your body changes from this moment on, this foundation must always remain. The goal is no longer to perfect your body; instead, it is to get to know and understand your body by creating a loving, caring, positive environment in your mind.

By choosing yourself, you accept that you are deserving of your body and of your existence here on earth. You allow yourself the right to feel comfort and security, knowing you are never alone, and you are always loved and cared for. In addition to these benefits, you will not believe the resilience to face life's challenges this will cultivate.

Through this new understanding, you give yourself an opportunity to experience beauty from the inside out. You give yourself permission to reject a society that does not honor, love, and value all human beings as equal. You no longer accept unhealthy and negative people, thoughts, or energy. By choosing yourself, you choose authentic health by allowing your physical body to be a living expression of the real you that radiates goodness, positivity, and love into the world.

Most important, by choosing yourself, you accept the role of "gardener" and the responsibility of pulling out any weeds that pop up and threaten to overrun the beautiful garden that is your mind! You accept that you must tend to your garden every day to provide the proper nourishment needed for your newly planted seeds to grow. You must protect your garden from any and all things that seek to harm it, and you must take pride in and celebrate the beauty as it begins to bloom. Without the gardener helping create the right conditions, the garden cannot grow, and without the garden, the beauty the gardener enjoys ceases to exist. They are interdependent and need each other to thrive.

■ ■ ■

In Chapter 12, we take loving our bodies to the next level. By the "next level," I am talking about *action*. To love and appreciate your body is an important first step. But now that you are no longer judging and criticizing your body, you can succeed in bringing it to its healthiest, happiest state—which is a natural, beautiful expression of your true self.

■ ■ ■ ■ ■

Chapter 12

Make Healthy
the New "Skinny"

Now that we love and appreciate our body as a faithful friend, we need to show that love and appreciation through our actions, by doing what is good for it. First and foremost, this means no longer trying to make our body conform to the skinny beauty ideal. What a relief not to have that pressure!

As with any habit or way of life, to let go of the negative beauty ideal, we need to replace it with something positive—a new pattern of behavior, a new goal to focus on and work toward. I am asking you to work really hard to break the programming you have been running that focuses solely on weight and size. I am going to help you download a new program that is about loving yourself with true wellness. Let's get started!

Why Choose Healthy instead of Skinny?

We at Healthy Is the New Skinny (HNS) use the term *healthy* to refer to the optimal state our body can achieve—and this is what I invite you to make your new goal. The change required in your thinking won't happen overnight because we have grown up with the Western beauty ideal, and it is rooted deep in our subconscious. The first step is to become aware of our thinking.

So, why is healthy the new goal, the new "skinny"? Because when our body is in a state of excellent health, we are more easily able to return to being our true self. When our body is healthy, our mind is healthier, too. Our whole being is balanced and can relax instead of being in survival and fear mode, which causes us to feel that we're not good enough and constantly need to prove ourselves worthy of acceptance and love. When we're healthy, we make better decisions for ourselves, which makes us healthier and happier still—contributing to a positive life cycle.

An added benefit of making healthy the new skinny is that this is a goal we can all achieve. Unlike the beauty ideal of skinny, health is a unique state for each of us, in a way that is organic to our individual body. As we've discussed, the goal of being skinny puts us in a position to fail over and over again. It also weakens our body, which weakens our mind, and we deserve better than that.

What Is "Healthy"?

So, what is "healthy"? With our new understanding of our body as a vehicle that faithfully carries us through life, we can look at what healthy really means. While we may think of health as relating only to the body, this view is limited. Health affects all aspects of ourselves: body, mind, and spirit.

Physical Health

When you think about the word *healthy,* you might picture a particular body or body type. However, while that person on the magazine cover with six-pack abs may be one image of physical health, it could also be an image of someone who is actually *unhealthy.* Remember, you can't tell just from looking at a person whether he or she is healthy. Health is not a particular size or shape. Health is a condition, a state of well-being where the body is in the optimal position to heal and repair itself and function at its highest and most vital level.

Mental and Emotional Health

We are not one-dimensional beings, and optimal health includes all aspects of who we are—both our physical vehicle and our thoughts and emotions. Our system is one inter-related whole, so our mental health—how we think; what we believe; and the mind-set with which we approach ourselves, others, and life in general—can affect our physical health, and vice versa. When we are not in balance, our emotional health—how we feel—can alter our mental health, which again affects our physical health.

What does good mental and emotional health look like? This will vary for each of us, as we all have different personality traits, thought processes, and social programming. I will use my husband and myself as examples. A classic Virgo, Bradford is always analyzing and planning things out in his mind. He is extremely detail oriented and likes to follow a plan. When he is out of balance mentally and emotionally, such as when he is unable to control his surroundings, these natural traits can turn to extreme self-criticism and anxiety.

I am a Pisces, the opposite sign of the zodiac. I am naturally free-spirited and don't need a plan at all. I actually do well just going with the flow. I am extremely visually creative and always thinking about new ideas and projects. When I am not in balance, however, I can become overwhelmed and feel like I am drowning in a sea of things I need to get done. My perfectionism takes over and robs me of my creativity.

Life will always throw us out of balance at times. Good mental and emotional health includes the ability to recognize when you are out of balance. Then you can do what is necessary to bring yourself back into healthy function.

Spiritual Health

Spiritual health comes with living true to yourself and in alignment with your life purpose. It occurs when your mind, body, and spirit line up with your authentic self. When you begin to connect to your true self in health and wellness, you are more likely to be free of disease and dysfunction, have sustainable energy, and be functioning well. You are able to live a full, happy life with balance, harmony, and vitality. When you reach this state of being, you *know* that you are far more than just a body, and you allow yourself to discover what that means to you on a spiritual level—eventually expanding your thoughts on health to include all aspects of yourself.

When you become connected to your true self and begin to heal from the inside out, your focus shifts from yourself and your physical body to the world. Your thinking shifts from "me" to "we." When you make this shift, you notice that you are an important part of the world, and your choices affect not only you but also those around you and the environment. When you are spiritually healthy, you realize that you are connected to everyone and everything.

The Media's Representation of Healthy

As you ponder your own health, keep in mind that there is a difference between being physically healthy and physically "fit." Health and fitness are not the same thing, even though the media might have you believing differently. The media portrays healthy as being either skinny or fit, but not necessarily healthy in mind, body, and spirit. A "gym body" is not necessarily well, vital, in balance, and able to heal and repair itself. Remember that!

It is common in our society to be complimented on your body when it looks similar to the images portrayed in the media. In fact, I have heard from countless girls and women that they received the most compliments about their appearance when they were in the depths of their eating disorders, literally killing their bodies from the inside out. That is a great example of how our cultural view of what is ideal can be so damaging.

As we focus on being healthy, we need to be hyperaware of how the media attempts to sell us products we don't need. The media's ideal of fitness and health looks remarkably similar to the beauty ideal, with a narrow definition and associated image—very low body fat, six-pack abs, and the "right" amount of muscles. This limited image of health fuels the sale of products. For example, according to ABC News, the weight-loss industry in the United States makes roughly $20 billion a year from diet pills, diet books, and weight-loss surgery. From supplements and waist trainers to diet tea, it is hard to walk down the street or scroll through your social-media feed without seeing some kind of advertisement for weight loss.

On the other hand, obesity is a growing concern in our society. The percentage of adults in the United States who were obese in 2014 was 27.1 percent, representing an upward trend from 25.5 percent in 2008. Interestingly, the prevalence of eating disorders has also increased, as tracked by studies over the last 50 years. These statistics indicate that a significant portion of our society is extremely unhealthy. Moreover, a lack of education mixed with the media's limited depiction of health is harmful to us all.

Healthy Comes in All Shapes and Sizes

The truth is that when you go out in public, you see few people who match our cultural beauty ideal, if any at all. Participating in my first half-marathon (I walked/ran), I was so surprised at the vast differences in the body types I saw. There were people of every shape and size, from the very lean to people who were 300-plus pounds. A guy passed me on his prosthetic legs, running like the wind. I saw so many amazing people come together to challenge themselves and do something that was physically active on a beautiful day.

Want to know what I did not see? I didn't see a single woman who had the fashion model body type. Now, there might have been a few in the mix, but I didn't see any. In fact, I bet you too will have a hard time finding the bodies you see in advertisements in real life. Ask yourself why you are not allowing yourself to be inspired by the beauty all around you—the people you know and see in real life. Why are you only being taught to look like what you see on a screen or on paper? Does that make sense to you?

So we know we don't spot models left and right when we are going about our daily lives, but we do see a lot of people who are overweight. I think we need to address the fact that being overweight, just like being underweight, is not a state of optimal health. This conversation is especially sensitive because one extreme is praised whereas the other is criticized. That is not what we are doing here. As I have said throughout this book, I understand both sides; I have experienced both praise for my looks and shame for my weight and size. These experiences have helped me come to the essential understanding that you will be judged no matter what. So you might as well choose health and focus on the things that make your mind, body, and soul feel amazing.

Achieving and maintaining a healthy weight for your height is a good starting point. What is a healthy weight? This is a gray area. Some use BMI, a measure of body fat based on height and weight, to determine if they are underweight, normal weight, overweight, or obese. The BMI calculator can be useful, but my measure is less about numbers and more about survival. I ask you, "How long would you last in the *zombie apocalypse*?" No, really. Does your body have enough fat reserves that you aren't going to die or be too weak to function going for periods of time without food? Are you in good enough condition to walk for long periods? Or are you weighed down and so out of shape that you wouldn't be able to outrun the zombies and make it to safety?

Recently I flew into Denver at the opposite end of the terminal from my connecting flight. I had to run with my bag from one end of an extremely long terminal to the other. I made my flight, but my lungs were burning and I was winded. I thought, *Damn, I need to do more cardio.* My body was telling me that I was not in optimal shape.

A really important point here is that I was at a healthy weight according to my BMI, but I was not *in shape*. Health is multidimensional—just like you are as a person. So when you assess your health, be sure to think about it in terms of what your body allows you to do: Can you run to catch the bus? Can you walk up 10 flights of stairs? Are you able to carry your own groceries or play with your kids without feeling exhausted? These everyday tasks represent quality of life, which must be considered in measuring your health.

What It Looks Like to Strive for Healthy

I post photos of women of all shapes on the HNS Facebook page because—despite the media messaging we are constantly bombarded with—many different body types can be representative of optimal health and wellness. One of the girls I've posted, Rose, is a model with my agency, Natural Model Management.

Rose is one of the nicest human beings I have ever met. She is one of those people who would never harm anyone. However, being happy and comfortable in her own skin has always been hard for Rose because she was tormented and bullied throughout her adolescence because of her weight. When I met Rose, I instantly liked her as a person and saw so much potential when it came to being a working model. The only problem was that she was size 18, and sample sizes for plus-size clothing are typically sizes 12 and 14.

When I signed Rose, it was clear that she was not yet comfortable with her body or herself in general. She would tug at her clothing and stand with her shoulders down and forward. She would also apologize all the time for absolutely no reason. One of her goals was to become healthier as a person, so I was happy to help in any way I could. Over the course of two years, I gave her numerous pep talks about health, the industry, what was going on in her life, and how—when she was ready—to let go of feeling guilty for existing.

One day everything I had said to her clicked, and she decided that she was going to make some changes. She set a goal of eating healthy and walking daily for 30 days. She stuck to her plan, lost 10 pounds that first month, and felt really proud of herself. She loved her new routine and was feeling happier and more energized, so she decided to keep going. She learned how to cook, and, as she got in better physical condition, discovered new ways to work out at the gym that challenged her. After eight months, Rose lost 60 pounds and went from size 18 to size 14.

As a result of making this lifestyle change, Rose quickly realized that her weight and physical health weren't the only things contributing to her unhappiness. She realized that her marriage was not working for her. Her needs were not being met, and the stress and animosity in her relationship with her husband were having a negative effect on her mind and spirit. She knew she had to make the difficult choice to separate from her husband and allow space in her life to focus on herself, trusting that doing so would attract a healthy, positive relationship in the future.

I can't tell you the difference I have seen in this woman as a result! She is vibrant and beautiful, and she now stands with her head up and shoulders back and no longer apologizes for being in the room or on the planet. She is sweet and silly and has so much fun no matter where she is. I believe she finally found her way back to her true self.

Haters Gonna Hate

If you do not fit the picture of "health" in our society, then you may be labeled lazy, out of shape, fat, or worthless. I see these harsh judgments firsthand on the HNS Facebook page. I post only photos and stories of women on our page who are living an active, healthy, positive lifestyle, so I'm always confused by the negativity and judgmental comments. It may be that those who are being so critical have yet to become aware of the unconscious programming that has shaped their opinions. They can see only one narrow definition of beauty, and completely miss the true component of "health."

When I posted a photo of myself in a bikini to promote our brand's swimwear, the comments were all positive. So I was excited to post photos of Rose; our high-waist bikinis fit her like a glove, and she looked amazing in them. I simply couldn't believe the nasty comments we received on social media: "This isn't healthy; this is fat." "I guess fat is the new skinny." "Promoting obesity is wrong." "This page shouldn't promote obesity."

I instantly felt anger. This photo shoot was the first time Rose had put on a bikini, let alone taken photos in one. She saw the photos before I posted them and thanked my husband and me for taking them because she felt so beautiful and proud of her body. It made me sick to my stomach to think of Rose reading those comments. Rose didn't deserve that; no one deserves that! And the comments weren't *true*! They were, at best, skewed because of a belief in the skinny beauty ideal, or, at worst, mean for the sake of being mean.

It is shocking to me that there are so many people who claim to hate obesity to the point that they feel the need to make cruel comments on a woman's photo without knowing anything about her or her story. And it is so wrong that women who look healthy on the outside might be showered with compliments and praise even if they are sick and suffering from an eating disorder.

We all know that being overweight is linked with serious health conditions; I am not overlooking that fact at all. The message I *am* trying to convey is that there is no single look of "health" or "healthy." People looked at Rose's swimsuit photo and categorized her as unhealthy and overweight, when in reality she was doing all the right things for her body and was in amazing physical condition. It is ironic that people who are so against obesity would put down a person who just lost 60 pounds by changing her diet and working out! You would think those people would be celebrating Rose's lifestyle change and accomplishments by being kind and supportive versus cruel and judgmental.

Setting Healthy Goals

My personal health has been a roller-coaster ride that I am happy to say now has no more hills and valleys. Ask my husband, and he will tell you how much I hated the drops! I had to experience those ups and downs so that I could understand what balance is for me. After taking my body and health to the extreme, I realized that 140 was not my ideal weight even if it brought me closer to the skinny beauty ideal. Now I know the ideal weight for my frame is around 160 pounds—20 pounds heavier than my lowest and 40 pounds lighter than my heaviest. I feel strong, energized, happy, and comfortable in my skin; I never felt that way at my lowest or my heaviest weights.

I encourage you to think about when you were happiest and most comfortable with yourself. When did you feel your best in mind, body, and spirit? If your initial response is "never" . . . that is still great! Now you at least know what you are looking for, and you have an opportunity to discover that place for the first time. That is exciting.

I want you to know that there is nothing wrong with self-improvement, goals, or being thin and lean. We want to be our healthiest, whatever that looks like for our own body. We just need to shift our motivation from being skinny as a way to find value and acceptance, to being healthy so we can live our best life.

Making healthy the new skinny is not about the *body*; it is all about our *mind-set*. If you find yourself falling back into old patterns, just say out loud, "Healthy is the new skinny!" My husband holds me accountable if I am not practicing what I preach. He asks me, "Are you doing this because it is good for your body and relieves stress or because you want to be skinny?" Then I think, *Damn it*, and laugh, because he is right—and I need that perspective. This challenge to my subconsciously ingrained programming really helps me to regroup and start fresh with a positive outlook.

It is 100 percent okay to set goals for yourself when it comes to eating healthy foods and challenging your physical health. The primary thing to keep in mind as you create your goals is to evaluate whether they are coming from self-love or from self-loathing. Goals that are based solely on physical appearance do not come from self-love. They tend to come from a place of insecurity and dissatisfaction with yourself or wanting someone else's approval and acceptance.

I recently saw a new book with a title like *Hot Body Workout* and a subtitle along the lines of *Get Your Best Butt, Sexiest Abs, and Sexy, Strong Legs*. Immediately I recognized that this book was not going to provide any positive motivation for my mind, body, or spirit. In fact, this kind of book could pull me back into thinking health is all about how hot you are—aka the "I am not enough" mentality. To focus only on my body parts would mean I would be denying the other important aspects of myself and my health, which is something I no longer do.

I want you to do something different from this. I want you to choose action steps for health and wellness that relate to your quality of life. Depending on your current health, your goal might be to have more energy for basic tasks like raising your children or being on your feet all day at work. Or you might set a health goal that focuses on a particular accomplishment, such as what I do with weightlifting: I monitor the amount I can do, what my body is capable of, and how much I improve from week to week.

When you focus on optimal health as we have defined it in this chapter, your body changes on its own. There is no need to try to control or force it to be something it isn't. Let it evolve into what it is meant to be from a place of self-love and self-acceptance. You never know: you might end up with a tighter figure or outrageous curves or six-pack abs or stronger legs, but these will just be a bonus to the real prize of health and wellness.

■ ■ ■

Together we need to be more mindful of the judgments we make of others and ourselves. Both are unnecessary and, usually, not even accurate. If you find yourself judging others and their bodies—whether the judgment is good or bad— take a moment to become aware of that thought. Then ask yourself, "Why did I just think that?" Finally, correct your judgment with a thought like, *Every woman has a story, and I don't know hers.*

I am so grateful to have been exposed to so many different types of women and to hear their stories. I've learned that whatever your shape—thin, curvy, athletic, plus-size—your body will be judged and criticized. That is a pain we all know well, and the practice must stop.

The only way to know whether a person is healthy is to be that person and live as they do. Since that is impossible, I ask that we all stop worrying about one another's health and voicing our opinions on the matter. I invite you to turn within—tune in to what your mind, body, and spirit need in the moment. We talk more about what that means in Chapter 13.

■ ■ ■ ■ ■

Chapter 13

Create Great Health

Ellyn Silverman, one of Healthy Is the New Skinny's nutrition experts, shared with me an interpretation of great health that I love: "When I think of healthy, I think of well balanced . . . mind, body and soul. A centered place that incorporates good food, laughter, getting some exercise, getting sleep, and feeling well rested in the morning. Healthy from a nutritional perspective means knowing when you are hungry, eating when you feel hungry, and not feeling guilt around what you are eating. Nourishing your body with foods that make you smile and bring you joy. Not obsessing about the whats, wheres, and whens around food . . . not using it to distribute power. Getting back to the original role foods play in our lives . . . to nourish."

Merriam-Webster's definition of *health* is more succinct, of course: "the condition of being sound in body, mind, or spirit; especially: freedom from physical disease or pain" and "the general condition of the body." While the dictionary definition of health acknowledges mind and spirit, it focuses more on the body. As I proposed, once you love and accept yourself, your body will respond with wellness. Still, we cannot ignore the very physical aspect of health—what we do with our bodies, how we treat them, and what we put into them.

Is everyone capable of having a healthy body? Yes, at least the healthiest body possible for that unique person. In my experience, there are three key components of creating and maintaining optimal physical health:

1. Recognizing and accepting that different bodies have different needs

2. Finding out what works best for *your* body, by observing and experimenting

3. Always approaching your body from a place of self-love

In this chapter, we address these ideas while not losing sight of the fact that the physical aspect of health cannot truly be separated from the mental and spiritual.

Different Bodies, Different Needs

Some aspects of health are universal. For example, cigarette smoke, both direct and secondhand, is detrimental to all humans. Being exposed to or ingesting toxins, hormones, or chemicals is dangerous for everyone. We all have the same basic needs for vitamins, minerals, water, and protein in order to have a body that is strong, healthy, and properly functioning. There are subtle differences from person to person, however. And because of these variations, there is no single approach to health that meets everyone's needs. The multibillion-dollar diet industry would like you to believe it has the solution for everyone, but that is not true.

As a child the concept that your body has individual needs is pretty abstract. We look at other kids and compare ourselves with them. In that scenario, there is a winner and a loser. However, it is possible for two eighth graders to be healthy when one weighs 125 pounds and the other weighs 89 pounds, depending on their individual characteristics. It is important to start discussing health early on and teach kids how to make good choices *specifically for them*.

What's Best for Your Body?

Listen to your own body. Being aware of what helps your body function well and what does not is crucial. Without consciously caring for your body, it can become out of balance and unhealthy.

Recently, after watching the documentary *Cowspiracy: The Sustainability Secret*, I decided to become a vegetarian and found that the lifestyle works great for me. My husband, however, who has a much higher need for protein than I do, noticed that he was experiencing muscle fatigue and weakness after going vegan. This is an example of how similar processes works differently for different people. He has had to make specific changes in the diet, like adding protein shakes frequently, to keep his body operating well.

A few other examples of food-related idiosyncrasies come to mind. People with celiac disease respond negatively to gluten, a component of wheat. Others, like a friend of mine, are lactose intolerant and get sick if they eat dairy products. Some have allergies to nuts that can actually be life threatening. Yet for the majority of people, gluten, dairy, and nuts are just a normal part of their diet. That is why you need to discover your "individual normal," which can be significantly different from what is normal for others. Eat what works for *your* body, to keep it healthy, strong, and feeling good.

There is also variation in how much sleep people need to be healthy. I like a solid 8 to 10 hours, but I know people who need only 4 or 5 hours to function well the next day. In the past, I didn't realize that people's sleep requirements were so different!

Moving your body on a regular basis is also necessary for good health. Getting physical exercise is good for your body, heart, and mind. It releases endorphins and other chemicals that help with mood and strengthens your bones and muscles. Running marathons is not needed, unless you want to and that makes your body feel good. But getting moving every day for 30 to 60 minutes is healthy for all bodies. The intensity of that movement is your choice and varies from person to person.

EXERCISE: EXAMINING YOUR HEALTH HABITS

This three-part exercise will help you identify what *your* body needs for optimal health. You may want to write all your answers down in your journal.

1. *Review the past:* Look back over your life and identify what did and did not create health for you. Did you feel strong and confident when you were boxing three times a week? Was there a time that you stopped drinking caffeine and you realized that you were much more relaxed afterward? As a child, were there any foods or activities that your parents encouraged or discouraged?

2. *Evaluate the present:* Examine your current habits and notice which ones are nourishing you and which ones are not helping you to be your best self. For instance, do you find that you have more energy when you do yoga regularly? Conversely, when you have a few glasses of wine at night, do you feel tired and bloated the next day? Try to be really honest with yourself. It can be hard to let go of habitual behaviors that seem to provide a sense of comfort.

3. *Create a healthy future:* Compare your lists of the past and present choices you made for your body. I think you know what to do next: Be sure to implement the good ones, and ditch the not-so-good ones! Your healthy future begins as soon as you commit yourself to giving your body what it needs—and actually do it!

Loving Yourself to Health

I have tried all kinds of diets over the years, and none of them worked for me long term. When you think about it, it is crazy that we loathe our bodies, do extreme things to change it, and constantly send it negative thoughts and energy—and then wonder why we don't see the change we want in our health or our weight!

After losing 50 pounds in a normal, healthy way and then falling into an unhealthy pattern of pushing my body past its natural weight to please others, I realized something was not right. I needed to step back and evaluate why I was not feeling well. I was doing all the things I was told to do to be healthy, but I was consumed with how I looked. I was spending all my time and energy trying to manipulate and control my appearance. I didn't feel healthy at all. I was exhausted and hungry all the time.

My experience with the pursuit of health had been extremely negative my whole life. For example, when I participated in organized sports, we were forced to run to exhaustion as punishment for not performing well enough at practice or at a game. After that I hated to run because I always felt as if I was being punished; it gave me a feeling of anxiety and failure. When I did lose weight, I felt a lot of fear again. I feared gaining the weight back because I felt as though I was not able to control my eating, and I worried that I would again become the version of myself that I was ashamed of.

I know I am not the only woman who has been unhappy with her weight, "got healthy," lost weight, and was still unhappy with her body. I realize now that I was using the appearance of health to mask my attempts to conform and seek approval from others. I made choices that I claimed were for my health but in reality were to look a specific way. I would eat or not eat specific foods to look skinnier or build muscle to meet the media image of health and beauty. I was operating on the fear of not being enough.

You postpone your life with thoughts like, *When I look good in a bathing suit, I'll go to the beach,* and, *When I lose 25 pounds, my life will be so much better.* Your life is here, now, in this present moment, and you have the opportunity to change your thinking and be happy and live fully in every moment.

My epiphany was realizing that even when I looked the way society said I should, I was denying myself the things I desired most—positivity, acceptance, health, joy, happiness, and love. I polluted the positivity that *real* health offers with expectations, perfectionism, scorekeeping, and negative thinking. If I had really been operating from a place of self-love, I would not have done half of the things I did to my body.

After the yo-yo of struggling to lose weight only to gain it back, I started to look at things differently. Instead of focusing on losing weight because I hated the way my body looked, I switched to honoring and helping my body get what it needed through what I was eating. Coming from a place of love changed my body and my life! I now eat healthy, natural foods because my body functions better on that type of fuel. Our bodies are the vessels that allow us to exist physically in this world. We should cherish them and treat them with love and reverence.

■ ■ ■

When you have sustainable wellness and energy, it isn't only your body that benefits. You are now in a position to do nothing less than achieve your real dream in life. First, you must get deeply in touch with your true self, actively love yourself, and discover your purpose. I guide you through this transformational process in Part III.

■ ■ ■ ■ ■

Part Three

HOW TO GET
STARTED BEING YOU

Chapter 14

Discovering
Your True Self

This part of the book is incredibly meaningful to me, because it is where I have the privilege of guiding you on an important personal journey—the journey to fulfilling your potential. First, I help you begin to discover your true self, which is more magnificent than you might even imagine. Upon seeing your true self, you will realize how absolutely lovable you are! I share practices for caring for your body, mind, and soul. With self-care and self-love, you will no longer be dependent on the love and acceptance of others and you will be able to understand your life purpose—the reason you are here. Based on this awareness, you can figure out your *real* dream—what you want to accomplish out there in the world as a reflection of your authentic self. Let's begin!

The Heroine's Journey

There is nothing more empowering than the path of discovering your true self and your life's purpose and dream. Every woman or girl can be the heroine of her own journey. The questions I pose to you are the following: Are you going to fulfill the potential that is within you? Are you going to think for yourself and pursue your own dreams? Or are you going to allow others to dictate what they want for you—to manipulate you into being someone they want you to be, for their own profit and gain? Are you going to believe that you embody greatness and love, or are you going to accept the worldview that you are "lesser than" or "not good enough" and keep yourself small?

Life is not about being lost and then found. We have feelings of being lost because we are disconnected from our true selves and our purpose, but we are not lost—we are simply in process. Life is an ongoing discovery process of experimenting, discerning your truth, and becoming the real you. It was during the lowest points of my life that I learned the most about who I was and what I wanted. I wasn't lost at all—even though it felt like it—I was just having experiences that allowed me to learn and grow.

Life is about continually discovering your truth and what is best for you, and then letting what you discover direct what you do! To reconnect to yourself, you must constantly be on a quest to know yourself and discover what matters to you. Then, when you recognize your calling, it is your duty to live and speak your truth. I believe this is why we are here. This heroine's journey begins with being the real you.

Be the Real You

I know this seems simple enough. What could be easier than being who you really are? But it's actually extremely difficult to accomplish, especially in our society today. As the poet E. E. Cummings wrote: "To be nobody-but-yourself—in a world which is doing its best, night and day, to make you everybody else—means to fight the hardest battle which any human being can fight; and never stop fighting."

Let me give you an example. Recently I spoke at a high school in Northern California and, as with all my events, at the end girls came up and talked to me. I cannot tell you how many girls said to me, "I am a Christian, but I believe that all people are deserving of love no matter if you are gay or straight, man or woman. People are equal." The topic of equality has been coming up more and more, which tells me there is a consciousness around it that many girls feel passionate about.

When I hear these types of comments at my events, I always ask the same question: "How do you know what you believe?" The girls pause, think for a moment, and respond, "I just know it in my heart." Right! *In our hearts.* That's where our truth is. Of course, we have been raised to question what we know in our hearts when it doesn't fit what we have been told to believe. It is time that we stop doing that.

So how do you start seeing yourself accurately, listening to your heart, and being the real you? First, realize that you can never discover who you are if you are busy trying to adhere to others' ideas of who you should be. What does it mean to conform in our society today? We know there are certain ideals that the media promotes and tries to get people to adhere to. And we all know some chameleons—people who morph who they are depending on whom they are around. Because they are always changing to be like those around them, you never quite know who those people really are or how they feel. In fact, it's likely that they themselves don't know!

A perfect example of this can be found in the movie *Runaway Bride*, with Julia Roberts and Richard Gere. The theme centers on knowing oneself, and the plot of the movie involves Richard's character figuring out why Julia's character has been engaged multiple times but always decides to bail at the last minute. He interviews all the different "victims"— the grooms she left standing at the altar—to discover what her problem is. When he asks each man how Julia's character prefers her eggs for breakfast, every man provides a different answer, believing she likes the same kind of eggs he likes.

On the surface you might say, "It's just eggs. Who cares?" But when we detach from who we are, we also put our preferences, goals, interests, and opinions to the side. This makes it easy to take on another identity, but of course that is not the real us; that is the version of ourselves we feel we need to be in order to be accepted and loved. And yet, even if others give us their approval, we never actually feel the true acceptance and love we crave because it's not directed at our real selves.

Let's look at more examples of conforming. Remember junior high school? Talk about not having a mind of your own! I remember calling my friends so we could all agree to wear the same thing to school the next day. Where was my sense of individuality and personal style? Did one friend in your group ever get mad at another, and even though you had nothing to do with it, you somehow were talked into being mad at that person, too? Yeah, I did that as well. Where was my own opinion and ability to say, "I can be friends with both of you. You are mad about something stupid that doesn't even matter and has nothing to do with me"? And what about high school? Think about times when you desperately tried to fit in. Or maybe it would be easier to think of the few times you didn't!

We must understand that we are raised to conform, and simply becoming aware of that is the first step in changing. Once you recognize the times in your life when you were not true to who you are at your core, you can start to examine why and get to the root of your need to fall in line. Let's use my junior high mean-girl drama as an example. In junior high, everyone lives with anxiety and fear because we want to fit in. I didn't say what I actually thought because I feared the girls would turn on me, and I would be the new outcast whom they wouldn't talk to for three days. It was easier for me to be quiet and go along than to stand up for what I believed in. Likewise, why did I always want to be skinnier? Again, because I was conforming to the beauty ideal out of the fear of not being worthy of love and attention the way I was.

Challenge Your Fear and Find Your Wings

Fear is the force driving conformity. If you are able to realize that and challenge that fear, you will release yourself from its grip. And, oh, you will be happier! It is time to let go of fear and find freedom.

Where does freedom reside? In our wings. The problem is that we forget we have them.

To me, wings are a symbol of strength, freedom, power, and femininity. If we have wings, we are no longer stuck in one place. We are able to go wherever we want without limitations, and I think every one of us can identify with the desire to be limitless.

Yet from a young age our wings are clipped so that we will remain grounded and can be controlled. We are placed into social systems, like school, that are built on conformity and operate on anxiety and fear. Being in an environment that puts so many limitations on who we are allowed to be makes us concerned with not fitting in and not being enough.

I can honestly say that the biggest mistake I have made in my 30-plus years on this planet was not all the years I spent wishing I could strut down the runway wearing those prized Victoria's Secret "Angel" wings; it was not realizing that I already have powerful, beautiful, and valuable wings of my own. It was losing sight of all the inner resources I had within me that gave me the ability to take off and soar.

I'd like to share with you one of my favorite poems, which has been attributed to Rumi. I feel that it perfectly captures who we, as women, are. These words bring a tear to my eye because they embody the struggle we all share, in our effort to "fly."

You were born with potential.

You were born with goodness and trust.

You were born with ideals and dreams.

You were born with greatness.

You were born with wings.

You are not meant for crawling, so don't.

You have wings.

Learn to use them and fly.

Recently I was digging through my desk and came upon a photo of myself from when I was about eight years old. I was an angel for Halloween, standing there proudly in my makeshift costume of a white leotard and the poufy slip skirt that I had taken off of one of my mom's dresses. There I was, just my beautiful, happy self, wearing wings. I know that image surfaced suddenly for a reason—to confirm my present-day understanding of myself. It was a reminder that I am not meant for crawling, because I already have wings. The same is true for you! It is only when you believe you do not have wings of your own that others are able to try to sell you theirs. But please believe me—you cannot purchase the kind of wings you desire. You can only recognize the wings you were born with, wipe off the layers of dust that have kept them hidden, learn how to use them, and begin to fly.

EXERCISE: FINDING YOUR WINGS

We recently hosted a body-image meditation for Healthy Is the New Skinny, and it was an eye-opening experience for the 60 girls and women who participated. In a guided meditation by my good friend Jeroen DeWitt, we asked the girls and women to use their imaginations and let their minds run free. We started with the group visualizing protective symbols such as crosses of light on the bottoms of their feet and across their chests, light coming out of the back of their heads like a swirling halo, and a diamond on their necks representing unconditional love. Then we asked the group to visualize wings coming out of their backs. We told them to make the wings at least six feet tall above their heads.

After we completed this section of the meditation, we asked the girls and women to share what they had experienced. One girl told us, "I just felt pure love and really happy." Another woman commented, "When you said to add wings, I gave myself wings. But then you said to make them over six feet tall, and I thought, *Wow, I need to make my wings bigger*. I think it is interesting that I automatically gave myself small wings when I could have given myself any kind of wings I wanted!" A girl in the front row said, "I felt really feminine yet powerful, which is kind of weird because I don't normally feel that way."

You can sense your own halo and wings by following the steps of this meditation:

1. Put on some relaxing music to drown out any distracting noises. Get in a comfortable position, either lying down or sitting.

2. Close your eyes and spend a few minutes focusing on your breathing. Take some deep breaths in and out.

3. Picture what your halo might look like. Imagine pure energy and light shining out of the back of your head. Maybe your halo is sparkly and colorful, or swirling around in many different coils. Let your imagination create without limitations.

4. Imagine yourself with wings. Get creative! What color are they? How do they feel to the touch? How big or small are they? How do they move? Imagine your wings in as much detail as possible. Spend 5 to 10 minutes really having fun with your visualization.

5. When you are ready, open your eyes and answer the following questions:

   • What kind of energy did you feel during the exercise?

   • Did visualizing yourself with a halo and wings change the way you see yourself now? If so, how?

> - Did imagining yourself with wings give you a sense of freedom?
>
> - Did having wings make you want to fly?
>
> Wings are a metaphor for real qualities that you possess: strength, freedom, power, and femininity. When you are feeling small, inferior, or under the control of others, I hope you will remember this exercise and the fact that you have wings that you can use to fly.

Recognize Your True Qualities

From a young age, I knew deep in my heart that I was different—in a good way. I always felt that my opinion was of value. I knew I was born with greatness and potential. Everyone is born with this potential for greatness; unfortunately, as we mature, our culture teaches us otherwise. I was lucky that my mother always encouraged and supported me in developing that potential.

I remember an incident when I was about five years old. One day, my mom and I drove by a homeless man on the side of the road. I asked why he looked so ragged, and she explained that he did not have a home or family to stay with and so he lived on the street. I burst into tears at the idea that he had to sleep outside alone and asked if we could get him some breakfast. At the time, my mother was raising two kids on her own while working and going to school full-time, so we had little to no money. Although we couldn't really afford it, my mom drove right to McDonald's and dug into the bottom of her purse for loose change. We then drove around for 20 minutes until we found the man and gave him the food my mom had purchased with her assortment of pennies, nickels, and dimes.

This memory tells me that before I was ever a mean girl in junior high choosing sides and trying to be just like every other girl, I was kind, compassionate, and full of goodness. My experience with the homeless man was my natural, authentic reaction to another human being who had been cast out of society. I wanted to help him, feed him, and show him that he mattered and was loved. *That* was the real me, and I strive to be that version of myself.

When you were born, your little body took all the time it needed to grow and develop. You were unable to communicate through words, but you could smile, laugh, and cry. When you were a baby, your brain was in some ways like a blank slate—in its original state, before being changed by your sensory experiences. You were not born hating yourself; that is something you were taught.

Remember: You were born with goodness. You were born with *greatness*. The next exercise will help you get in touch with the glorious qualities you were born with.

EXERCISE: RECLAIMING YOUR TRUE SELF

Why do you think babies make us smile with happiness? It is because they are pure love and innocence. Well, you are *still* pure love and innocence! Reconnect to that place within you—your true self—through the following steps:

1. Get out an old photo album or photo collection and select five of your favorite photos of yourself as a child. Find images that bring up memories of happiness for you. Select images that show your true personality and spirit.

2. Choose one photo to start with and, in a journal or new computer file, answer these questions about that photo:

- How does this picture make you feel?

- Why did you choose this photo?

- What do you love about yourself in this picture?

- What is one lesson you can learn from the child in this picture?

3. Repeat Step #2 for the remaining four photos.

I believe that children represent the purest form of love in our world. I don't need to see your photos to know that they shine with beauty, happiness, love, and that amazing energy you were born with. I want you to become aware of the beautiful spirit in those photos and to realize that it is still within you. No matter how bad you currently feel about yourself, you now have proof that you were not made to hate; you were made to love.

■ ■ ■

Once you become aware that your self-loathing is not a reflection of your true self but rather of negative programming, you are able to begin your journey toward your true dreams. In the next chapter, we examine self-love more closely, as a source for positive choices and actions.

■ ■ ■ ■ ■

Chapter 15

Choosing Self-Love

I hope at this point you feel inspired to consciously honor and develop into your authentic self so you can live the life you truly desire. Before you can choose a dream and a direction for your life, however, you must first choose self-love!

The world needs our love to heal itself, but we cannot love the world if we cannot first learn to love ourselves. When we are not operating from self-love, our dreams for the future won't be connected to our life purpose. Rather, our dreams will merely be an attempt to validate our existence, an effort to prove our lovability and worthiness of others' acceptance and approval.

We do not have to earn love or prove we are lovable. We are already lovable—because love is our divine essence. Remember that we were born with goodness, and this goodness is our true self.

Self-Love Takes Work

The way to choose self-love is by making it your new goal in life to nourish your mind, body, and soul. Self-love and self-care are the core of discovering your purpose and realizing your dreams. Yet how many times have you told yourself, "Okay, I am going to love myself and stop living an unhealthy lifestyle"? Then, inevitably, negativity found a way back into your thoughts and behavior. We have all been there!

I want you to know that self-love *is* possible; it just requires us to look deeper to discover who we really are. Because the truth is, when we know who we really are, we can't help but love ourselves.

I recently worked with a model named Lezah, who told me that she has struggled her whole life with liking herself. She's had bouts with eating disorders and has always struggled to have a healthy relationship with food. "A few seconds on the lips, years on the hips," her mother would tell her when she would eat snacks as a child. As Lezah shared her story with me, I couldn't help but pick up on the "glass-half-empty" view she had about actually liking herself one day.

"I know it is possible, but it just requires soooo much work," she told me. Yes, that is correct! If you want to change the toxic view you have of yourself, your body, and your place in the world—a view that is creating the majority of the misery in your life—you are going to have to work at it every single day until you suddenly realize that you have transitioned from negative to positive, self-abandonment to self-advocacy, and self-loathing to self-love. And, again, if only we could see ourselves as we really are—our true selves—it wouldn't be hard to love ourselves at all. This must be your goal.

Operating from Self-Love

When you find yourself falling into old patterns that pull you away from your new goal, and lead you to focus all your time and energy on your physical body, you need to stop and ask yourself, "Am I nourishing my mind, body, and soul? Am I making this choice to *better my health*, or to *be skinny* so I can be accepted?" By doing this you will be able to protect your well-being and overall health from the bombardment of media messaging that has been affecting your self-image and decision making up to now.

Every time you recognize that you are not thinking from a place of self-love, you always have the option to make a different choice. You have an opportunity to correct yourself and then choose self-love in that moment. That is your power of free will! Let's take a closer look at consciously loving and caring for your mind, body, and soul.

Mind

The practice of loving yourself begins with understanding that your spirit is not "lesser than" anyone else's. My spirit is not more or less valuable than my husband's spirit. Furthermore, we need to stop feeling guilty for making ourselves a priority. Every single person is entitled to their own self-care.

Misperceptions about our true selves—including being inferior, unworthy, and undeserving of love—lead to a negative life cycle. We must challenge the negative beliefs imposed on us by society, the media, and our loved ones and replace these negative thoughts with positive ones.

Always remember that you have the freedom to choose a positive thought over a negative thought, especially when it comes to your assessment of yourself. Do not accept the mean thoughts you have about yourself. Instead, remember what an innately loving, compassionate, good, and *great* person you are. Remember to speak to yourself with words that are True, Helpful, Inspiring, Necessary, and Kind (THINK). Talk to yourself as you would to a pure and innocent little girl—the one inside you.

By removing the fear, shame, and other negativity that you have allowed to cloud your perception of yourself, you are letting yourself have a *new* experience, one that is much more positive than the past. This experience can be exhilarating as you begin to really live your own life.

Body

It is not only your thoughts, beliefs, and self-talk that need to be fueled by self-love but also your behaviors—your diet, exercise, routines, other habits, and overall self-care. You cannot just think your body into health; you must take action. That means working out because you are honoring and caring for the needs of your body—and *not* working out because you hate your body and want to change it!

Fear and shame are common reasons to avoid exercise. There were so many times that I did not go to the gym or join a group activity because I worried that others were judging me as not fit enough to be there. That kind of thinking stems from the fear of not being enough. The sad thing is that people who are fit don't stare and laugh at others making an effort to better their health. I see people all the time at the gym who are working really hard but don't have a "gym body," and they are inspiring! I think, *You go, girl*. So moving forward, tell yourself, "This is where I am right now. I am capable of healthy changes. There is no shame in my game!"

When we make choices from a place of self-loathing, even supposedly healthy actions cannot contribute positively to our well-being. Think: when you make food choices from a place of love, what should you be conscious of? (Other than the fact that you are "hangry"!) Start thinking of the things you are putting into your body as your source of fuel. Ask yourself, "Does this food give me sustained energy? Does it make my body feel well?" If the majority of your diet provides your body with nutrients and energy, and you have a few not-so-nutrient-rich foods that you enjoy, you are eating in a balanced way that you can stick with. One piece of pizza isn't going to make you unhealthy, in the same way that one salad or plate of steamed vegetables isn't going to make you healthy.

Recognize that when it comes to your nutrition, you have free will to eat whatever you would like. Then make choices that are from a place of self-love. No restriction, no rules, no diets, just a principle of eating food as an act of self-love to nourish your body as a vehicle for your heart, mind, and soul.

As you begin to set new goals for your physical health, make sure to focus on what your body is capable of and feel grateful for its accomplishments. For example, I love to lift weights, and I enjoy setting new goals to strengthen my muscles. I have removed expectations of how my body "should" look and instead focus on the things my body is *capable* of. I feel grateful and proud of myself. It doesn't matter what the scale says, because when you live your life from an authentic place of self-love, your body will reflect that over time.

Remember, your body is not here to meet the expectations of others—it is a gift to enable you to live! When you are in touch with your body and you allow it to be as it was created, you are giving it an opportunity to evolve into a living expression of the real you. It didn't take you one week to become unhealthy, and it is going to take more than a week to become the living expression of health and happiness you desire to be. The keys here are patience, acceptance, self-love, and gratitude.

Soul

In addition to caring for your mind and body, you must nourish your soul, or spirit—the very essence of who you are. On a very practical level, you should evaluate and examine your daily schedule and routine. Are there changes you could make to allow more time for self-care, including quiet relaxation? How might you adjust your routine to be more enjoyable and uplifting? Sometimes that requires saying no when you are all booked up or letting go of activities and obligations that are largely depleting you. The time you give yourself for self-care should not come after meeting other people's needs. If you do not care for yourself, then you won't be able to effectively be of service to anyone else.

The health of your soul also depends largely on your relationships with others. The people you choose to spend time with have a profound effect on your energy and the way you feel about yourself. I suggest taking a closer look at your friendships and asking yourself if they are healthy, positive relationships. It is so easy to keep people around who don't contribute much to your life simply because they have always been there or you fear conflict or feel guilty for moving on or have a sense of obligation to keep them in your life. When you operate from a place of self-love, you understand the tremendous importance of protecting the positive environment you are working so hard to create. What you once tolerated from others and viewed as normal may begin to change. It's important to recognize when a friendship has run its course.

People often want to be friends with me for what I can offer them, such as a modeling job, free pictures, pep talks, knowledge, and the perks that go along with my lifestyle. As I became aware of what qualities I admire in others—including ambition, passion, kindness, loyalty, honesty, sense of humor, goodness, positivity, and just an overall pleasant energy to be around—it became obvious to me which "friends" were lacking. I noticed which people would only come to me with their problems, or needing something, or to complain or gossip about others. It also became clear that, despite my efforts, I could not help those people in any meaningful way, that they have to help themselves—and I was no longer willing to invest my time and energy there.

When you operate from a place of self-love, you value your time and energy. You start to feel the need to protect it from those who only take and never give in a way that makes you both healthy and strong. Healthy friendships are not one-sided; they are a balance, with each person contributing to the other.

When you disconnect from the people who constantly drain your time and energy but never give anything in return, you create space in your life for new energy and friends who are going to contribute positively to your life experience and goals. For example, we had our first Re-Model Me event to teach about healthy body-image and media manipulation, and around 40 girls and women came. The most amazing part of the event was seeing these women—all with the goal of becoming the best version of themselves—connect! After the event, we would see photos of participants hanging out and tons of comments back and forth between them on social media, spreading positivity and encouragement. When you discover what you truly like and then go out and do those things, you will find like-minded people who share your passions and interests.

When you consciously evaluate your life and your choices leading up to this point, you may realize that there have been relationships that were not healthy for you. You may even be in a relationship right now that you know is not supporting you in operating from a place of self-love. I didn't say this was easy; in fact, I reminded you that being yourself in a world that tells you who you should be will be your greatest accomplishment. Just like you cannot smoke and be truly healthy physically, you cannot be in a toxic relationship and be happy or healthy in life. It is impossible.

The only reason we stay in relationships that are not beneficial to our well-being is because we do not feel deserving of better. We fear we are unlovable and will end up alone. This is where self-love comes in. When you love yourself, you cannot feel alone. Self-love and the fear of being unlovable cannot coexist because when you operate from a place of self-love, *you* have decided that you are lovable.

Self-love is a game changer because you will be present in a relationship only when you both benefit from it; if not, there is not a good reason to be there. The following exercise will help you evaluate whether you are making choices from self-love; these choices include those you make in relationships.

EXERCISE: MAKING CHOICES FROM SELF-LOVE

To help you stay true to yourself and act from self-love, do this exercise for evaluating your choices. When you feel as if you don't know what to do in a situation, ask yourself the following questions:

1. "Does this choice honor my true self?"
   - *(If the answer is not a resounding yes, ask yourself the following question.)*

2.   "Will this choice make me healthier and happier?"
   - *(If the answer is not a definite yes, ask yourself an additional question.)*

3.   "Am I making this choice out of self-loathing, because I hate some aspect of myself?"
   - *(If the answer is not a firm no, ask yourself one more question.)*

4.   "Am I making this choice out of a desire for the acceptance of others?"
   - *(Again, the answer should be no.)*

The answers to these questions will give you all the information you need to make the best choice for yourself. By asking yourself what is best and listening to your own inner guidance, you are taking control of your life and its outcomes! In the following section, I share the stories of several women who did just that.

Role Models for Choosing Self-Love

Cassandra, a woman who came to one of our Re-Model Me events, told me and my husband that we helped her realize something—when her husband tells her she is beautiful, she is allowed to believe him! She said she would undermine her relationship because she was so insecure, even though her husband would always tell her she is perfect the way she is.

Another woman I have encouraged to believe in herself for the past few years, Mellie, has made huge changes to her lifestyle. Once she began to operate from a place of self-love, she also wanted to care for her body. She lost more than 70 pounds in the past year and is feeling better than she has ever felt.

Furthermore, as a result of her consciously honoring herself, Mellie realized that her marriage was not a healthy relationship. While she loved her husband as a person, she had married the first man who paid her attention because she feared no one else would ever love her. Because of that, she'd married a person with whom she did not have much in common. Now Mellie realized that they both needed to be set free to find the soul connection that she now understood could come from a partner.

Another friend of mine, Ani, struggled with the guilt of disappointing her family, who wanted nothing more than for her to find a husband and have kids like her brothers and sisters had done. Yet here she was in her 30s and she'd never even had a boyfriend! She felt so much anxiety over the pressure from her family and her religion that it actually stopped her from welcoming those experiences she desired into her life.

With a little coaching and time to reflect, Ani was able to slowly start loving herself for all her great gifts. She began to scrutinize the beliefs she'd been taught about love and relationships to understand why something that can be such a wonderful aspect of life could cause her such negative emotions. After taking time to connect to what she really valued and believed and to see her own beauty, she made some serious changes to her life. She began seeing a therapist to talk out some of the feelings she had kept inside for so long. She began lifting weights at the gym. She embraced her fun, geeky side and made efforts to connect with like-minded people who shared the same interests and also had goals of health and well-being.

I am so happy to report that, after doing this hard work for over a year, Ani is in a healthy, loving relationship with an amazing man she met at Comic-Con, a convention that celebrates comics and "nerd" culture! They truly are a wonderful match, and had she not gone down that road to self-discovery and put in the personal work required to become her best self, she never would have allowed herself the opportunity of a loving relationship. More important, she never would have discovered and begun living her truth.

Can you see how this is all connected? How you feel about yourself dictates the choices you make. The choices you make and the energy you embody attract positivity or negativity into your life. The foundation of health and happiness and truly all things positive is self-love. Before you can attract what is going to be good for your body, mind, and soul, you must choose to love yourself.

■ ■ ■

Indeed, the bedrock of a positive life is self-love. One reason self-love is so vital is that it is the key that opens the door to discovering your purpose—why you are here. In Chapter 16, I share what I have learned about this profound stage of the heroine's journey.

■ ■ ■ ■ ■

Chapter 16

Discovering
Your Purpose

In my work, as I have mentioned, I have met thousands of girls and women. Like me, they have all felt as if they were meant to do meaningful things in life but couldn't overcome the feeling of being lost. When people feel lost, what they're really doing is asking, "What is my purpose? Why am I here?" Believe me—if you knew and understood your purpose, you would not feel lost.

The good news is that your purpose is inside you, and it can never be lost—although it can be hidden, largely by the societal and familial programming we discussed earlier. You have already taken two fundamental steps toward uncovering your purpose: you have discovered your true self, and you have shifted your perception of yourself to love. This shift to self-love has freed you from the need to validate your worth and existence from the outside. Seeking the approval of others seemed to be your purpose before. But liberated from this false goal, you can now find your true purpose.

I was not born to be beautiful or to be a figure for others to lust after or stare at. I am a much larger entity of which my physical body and appearance are only a small, insignificant part. That is true for all of us. Finding your purpose may sound like a lofty goal, and it does take conscious effort and self-awareness. But it does *not* have to be a great mystery. In this chapter, I offer some guiding principles.

Please take my words to heart. I found my life purpose, and I feel so lucky to be able to live it every day. I know you can do it, too. Once you have connected to your true self and are making choices from a place of self-love, you can then discover and create your true dream—a vision for your future that emanates from who you really are.

Stay True to Yourself

Earlier we talked about discovering your true self; now it is time to stay true to the self you discovered by connecting to your free will—your power to *choose*. You may worry that your choices will alienate those around you. Others might become hostile to you or even reject you for not conforming to their ideas about how you should think and act. The antidote to this fear and to conformity in general is being yourself, regardless of the fallout. This requires you to release your fear of judgment, and challenge the programming that taught you to conform in the first place. It also entails building a safe place within yourself that is your home—full of self-love, kindness, and self-acceptance. Think of it as building a strong core. Every time you work to better yourself and understand who you are, that core gets stronger and stronger. Eventually when people throw negativity your way, it will no longer have the same damaging effect because your core will keep you standing tall.

When it comes to your future and creating a dream for your life, you have to promise yourself that you will trust what you feel is best. Always. Even when others do not understand you or you don't quite know where to go from one decision to the next. You have to listen to your inner guidance that pulls you toward your purpose, and then you must act on that intuition.

Doing this is difficult and lonely at times. It can be rough if you follow your path and others do not approve of your choices or try to sabotage you. People in your life will fall away, and new people will enter. If you remain positive, the new people will provide the help and support you need at the perfect time. You will know you are on the right path when you have feelings of happiness, joy, peace of mind, relief, and bliss. As long as you make choices that result in that outcome, you are on the road that's true for your life and that will create a beautiful future.

Nowadays, I know my truth, live my truth, and speak my truth without fear of rejection. This is a wonderfully secure, peaceful, and fulfilling place to be. You can never be alone if you have your *own* support, which is one of the most amazing things I have learned so far. Everything you need is already within you; now is the time to discover and develop it!

Embrace Your Feminine Spirit

Part of discovering your purpose is accepting that you are connected to a higher power of love and goodness. It runs through you, and you can be a living expression of that love and goodness here on earth. That's what you were meant to be! Anytime you wish to put love into the world and others tell you that is wrong, you should question it. Connecting to your goodness and to love allows you the opportunity to discover what your life purpose is.

I truly believe that feminine energy represents the purest form of love on earth, and that the female spirit is dying as a result of the ongoing assault against women in various forms around the world today. When we look at the world, there seems to be an absence of love. Together, we can restore the love the world needs.

The world needs a balance of both masculine and feminine energy. Masculine energy is powerful, protective, independent, and self-confident, while feminine energy is nurturing, warm, affectionate, and maternal. These are generalizations, of course, and we all—males and females alike—have both masculine and feminine traits in different proportions.

As women, if we choose to express our female spirit, we are choosing to provide love and positivity to ourselves and to the world. Although the power of love we possess is not physical, it is the greatest power of all. Love is all that we are and all that we need, and being in touch with love will help you find your purpose. You may not be ready to make this leap yet, but I would argue that sharing the love inside us with the world is everyone's purpose. It is our individual expression of how to do this that makes each of us unique.

Use Your Struggles

Think about the struggles you have been through. Although you may not have realized it while you were going through them, hard times can motivate you to contribute to the world. I realize now that while I was feeling lost, I was gaining perspective and experience that assisted me in discovering my truth and purpose in life.

When I talk to girls and women who have struggled with eating disorders, I like to point out that our culture is creating this sickness that is not natural to who we are. And it is getting worse. Over the last several decades, the incidence of eating disorders among children and teens has risen steadily. So many girls who struggle with these illnesses cannot see that their struggle is also part of their purpose. Who can better inspire the new generation of girls to know they can recover more than a girl who has made it through?

The girls who have suffered and recovered have the ability to help eradicate the cause of their disease, as well as to assist others in healing. At this time in our society, that is an incredibly important purpose. It is the same with women who once suffered from self-hatred and expressed that physically by being overweight—and then turned that around into self-love and achieved a weight that was healthy for them. We all have the potential to inspire greatness in others and to improve the harmful aspects of our society. It starts with changing ourselves. Remember, changing our energy changes the energy around us. If each of us changes in positive ways, the world will follow. The critical first step is that we connect to and begin to live our life as our true self.

By connecting to your true self, you accept your life's difficulties and the lessons they provide and understand they were given to you to serve your higher purpose—which, in turn, helps you serve the world.

Experience, Explore, Experiment

You are not going to receive an e-mail or a Facebook message from your higher self explaining your life purpose. You must go out into the world and, through experiences, begin to notice the special gifts you contribute to others. To find these gifts, look to your inspirations, aspirations, passions, and joys. The things we contribute to the world come to us naturally. They make us feel calm, happy, and satisfied. Yet sometimes we ignore them or choose not to value them because society has told us they are useless.

In high school, for example, I had a notebook in which I would sketch ideas for a clothing line. I thought it was a great idea to change the names of the sizes from "small," "medium," "large," and so on, to positive sayings. Looking back now, I can't believe it took me so long to realize that I knew part of my purpose long before I recognized it!

Think of yourself as a scientist or explorer whose goal is to experiment and discover what brings you the most passion, excitement, and energy. The process of finding your purpose can be exciting and fun if you approach it this way. For example, I wanted to get better at drawing, so I would take art classes, even though I was nervous because I didn't know anyone in them. Through doing this, I discovered that I enjoyed the peacefulness I felt while creating art. I moved to New York to model, and even though I didn't like it, I met one of my best friends and my husband on a trip to L.A. for work, which tells me that I was right where I was supposed to be at that time! I started new businesses, and, even though they are successful, I am always changing my understanding and trying to evolve to refine my purpose and improve myself.

Fear Not

When I was in high school, I was scared of everything. I used to joke with my mom and say it was because I watched too many Lifetime movies as a kid. You know, the movies where kids get abducted, or a stranger tries to kill the mom, or a natural disaster traps the kids somewhere. The first thing that would pop into my mind about things that were adventurous was, *I would never do that!* I said I would never do the bridge climb in Sydney, Australia, after seeing it on the show *The Amazing Race.* I said I would never go scuba diving because it was too scary. I said I would never do a half-marathon because it would be too hard. I said I would never ride a roller coaster because I hate speed and heights. I have done all of those things and enjoyed them all! Well, almost all—I won't be going on more roller-coaster rides anytime soon, but I am proud of myself for doing it that one time.

You can't "live true" and play it safe at the same time. When you decide that you deserve the opportunity to discover who you are outside of who the world tells you to be, you soon realize that life is meant to be an adventure. People take notice of how Bradford and I "live the life," as they say. We do what we love, we make our lives adventurous and fun by creating our own rules, and we stay away from people and things that don't contribute positivity. It is that simple.

Nurture Your Passion

Once you find your passion and joy, which are indicative of your calling or purpose, it is your job to cultivate them! It is necessary to do things each day to develop them. You must create the conditions for the great work of your life to emerge and evolve.

I think about and work on my purpose all day because I have created a business that promotes what I believe in. I find myself constantly learning and diving deeper into the task at hand. I love creating the visual content for our website by art-directing the photo shoots and creating the entire brand image by selecting the photos and creating the graphics. This work connects my creative side, which to me is fun and exciting, to Healthy Is the New Skinny's core message, which is my purpose.

You, too, can find your purpose. And when you find it, be sure to direct your positivity and energy there. Remember that energy creates more of the same energy and experiences via sympathetic vibrational resonance. Sometimes this is called a self-fulfilling prophecy; what you think about, you will attract. Only when you discover and begin to live from your truth can you attract what you truly desire.

Listen to Your Intuition

Intuition is that sense of knowing what is right for you, the right thing to do, the right decision to make. This inner guidance is the voice of your true self, which you can choose to follow or deny.

I once heard author Sonia Choquette describe listening to your intuition in the following way, which resonated with me deeply. You know when you are home alone at night and you hear a noise? You freeze, hold your breath, don't make a sound, and just listen . . . That is the kind of listening you need to be doing when it comes to your intuition.

I often reflect on Sonia's words because my mind never stops chattering! Ideas and thoughts run through my brain 24-7. When I became aware of this, I realized that I needed to take time out to quiet my mind and listen to my intuition. This meant creating ways of calming and slowing down my thoughts so I could receive the inner guidance I needed for the task at hand. I have found that meditation allows me to accomplish this.

When I first learned about meditation, I did not understand what it was all about. I was sitting there in a class full of people, listening to chimes and smelling incense, quiet on the outside but bored to tears on the inside. Most likely I had some kind of inappropriate commentary going on in my mind about the whole situation. That's because I didn't understand the very purpose of meditation, which is simply to take a moment to relax and reconnect with your true self, your intuition, and the good energy of the world. Once I realized that, I was able to let go of my perception of meditation and truly experience it.

I've also discovered that there are many ways to meditate. I find creative activities like painting and drawing to be extremely relaxing and an opportunity to connect back into myself. The major way that I feel connected and at peace is to immerse myself in nature. For example, I meditate when Bradford and I take our four-wheelers into the desert and find a place to stop and look out over the landscape. When I swim in the ocean, I feel that I am able to connect most easily to my true self and the energy of the world. In Mexico, where Bradford and I live for part of the year, I will just float in the waves for hours, just taking time to feel the beauty all around me. I feel so at peace and fulfilled.

Each one of us can take time every day to connect to our true self and the positive energy of the world. This practice can heal your wounds from years of negative thinking and provide you with a feeling of being loved and complete. It will also enhance your intuition, increasing the volume and frequency of the communication from that inner voice.

I love the idea I once heard that there is no hatred in our world, only the absence of love. There is no darkness, only the absence of light. There is no negativity, only the absence of positivity. When you are feeling an absence of love, light, or positivity, take time to stop and reconnect to these things that are always there for all of us.

■ ■ ■

Ultimately, we all have the same life purpose: to share our love and gifts with the world. The way we go about doing this—the way we express our purpose—is different for everyone, based on our unique interests and abilities. We talk more about this in Chapter 17.

■ ■ ■ ■ ■

Chapter 17

Finding and Pursuing Your Real Dream

In previous chapters, we talked about discovering your true self, loving yourself, and finding your purpose. These are necessary and important steps in rejecting society's programming—specifically, the programming that if you adhere to society's beauty ideal, you will have value. Once you have relinquished this false dream, however, where do you go? What do you seek then?

I have good news for you: you can seek anything you desire, whatever fulfills and inspires the real you. There are as many dreams as there are people! Maybe you have come to realize that, deep down, your purpose is to help people and alleviate their suffering; your dream might be to become some kind of healer. Maybe you want to devote yourself to empowering girls and women, like I do. Maybe your dream is to eradicate hunger, to bring clean water to villages in developing nations, to be a mother, to be an artist, to be a doctor, or to open a bakery. Maybe *several* of these dreams resonate with your authentic self!

As of this writing, I am the only person in the United States who files taxes as both a model and the owner of a modeling agency. I manifested a dream that had *yet to exist* in the entire country. To me, that is really cool. It has given me a nice boost of confidence as I continue to create a future for myself. I want you to know that just because a dream doesn't *currently* exist, that doesn't mean it *can't*. If you believe in something enough and it is true for you—mind, body, and soul—then the world is waiting for you to make your dream a reality. The first step is to stop following someone else's dream for you.

Don't Conform to Someone Else's Dream

When you begin to follow what feels right to you, you may have to *actively* reject or overcome what others tell you is your purpose or your dream in life. The difference between adopting a dream someone else dictates and creating your own is that the first puts you in a position where you have to conform, while the second offers you the opportunity to discover, develop, and unfold.

You'll know that your dream is authentic and coming from your soul when it does not require you to alter your body, mind, or soul in order to live that dream. That doesn't mean there won't be areas where you'll want to grow and improve, but your dream should never require you to starve your body, keep your mind weak, or make your spirit small. This is why modeling in the traditional sense is not an authentic dream for most people, because it would require them to harm their bodies, minds, and spirits in the pursuit and attainment of that dream. Authentic dreams that come from within will nourish your body, excite your mind, and fulfill your soul.

As a society, we seek validation and acceptance from others through the "dream" of being famous—for nearly anything! Just look, for example, at all those truly terrible singers who auditioned for talent competitions on TV, fully believing that they were meant to be pop stars. The reality is that many of those people were not following their unique gifts and honoring their life purpose. They chose fame as their "dream" because of the attention, happiness, popularity, acceptance, and love that the show promised to the select few. If the tone-deaf competitors were in touch with their true selves, they wouldn't squander their precious time and energy on something that is not going to serve them or the world. (Of course, I'm not saying they shouldn't sing for their personal enjoyment or expression. The shower is perfect for that!)

There are many variables and influences that push people in any given direction when it comes to their life plans or dreams for the future. The media plays a huge role, as does family. Parents often put a lot of pressure on their children to fulfill the vision they have for their lives. Perhaps the parents have a very specific view of success, like being a doctor, or perhaps they want their children to do the same things they did, like play the same sports or pursue the same career. Parents, please remember that your children are not mini versions of you! Yes, sometimes a child's purpose in life may be the same as or similar to a parent's, but more often than not it won't be.

My brother, Evan, followed his dream to be a doctor. He loves his career and is great at it. I, on the other hand, went in a totally different direction, leaving college early and starting my own businesses. Both of us are successful, yet not remotely in the same way. I can't imagine how terrible I would have felt about myself if my family had pressured me to be like Evan and continue with school when I knew with every fiber of my being it was not my right path. That one choice alone would have sent me down a negative road because I would not have been in a healthy environment that honored my style of learning and my purpose. Being able to honor each person's talents and strengths promotes self-love and success. It's not about right or wrong; it's about what is right for *you*.

It is time to stop waiting for others to give you permission to do what your heart knows is true. It is no one else's right, privilege, or responsibility to make sure you are living a healthy and happy life. That is your right, privilege, and responsibility because you are the author of your story, and it is up to you to choose how you fill the pages of your life. There is no right or wrong path, there is only the one you authentically discover and choose for yourself.

Challenge Your Dream

When you follow a dream blindly, you run the risk of your dream not reflecting the real you. False dreams can have many forms, too. For example, perhaps all the women in your family have been teachers, and it is assumed (even by you) that you will become one, too. Maybe everyone in your social circles is expected to go to Ivy League colleges, and this idea is so ingrained in you that you can envision nothing else for yourself. If you do not examine such dreams to see if they support your purpose and true self, you may spend a lot of time and energy pursuing a goal that is destined to leave you unhappy, unfulfilled, or even unhealthy.

As I've pointed out, modeling was not a dream I created for myself; it was one society told me was of value and that I should have. Like so many other girls, I accepted being a model as my dream without giving it any thought, with the unconscious belief that it would bring me love and acceptance. To adhere to industry standards, I, like many girls, resorted to unhealthy measures. When I tried to change myself to fit what others wanted me to be, my experience became extremely unhealthy for my body, mind, and spirit.

After years of modeling at a professional level, working in the industry as an agent, and interacting with hundreds of other models, I gathered enough information to challenge the belief that physical perfection equals value and gained the opportunity to create a dream of my own that was inspired by my unique gifts, abilities, and true calling in life. Though I may not book as much work as I would if I were to gain or lose 50 pounds, remaining the size I am now is the only way for me to have a healthy experience in the business. That is something I will never sacrifice again.

Although it may sound as though I believe to the contrary, when it comes to modeling as a whole, I am not entirely against it. To me, modeling is similar to beauty; it isn't modeling per se that is the problem, it's the limited criteria defining what a model is and should be that causes so much harm. Within the industry girls go to unhealthy lengths to meet the criteria so they can work. Outside the industry girls compare themselves with models who meet this criteria and always feel as though they are never enough. It's destructive almost every way you turn.

This leads me to again push you to reevaluate this "dream." Where did your dream come from? How do you expect to feel when you accomplish it? Who benefits if you achieve your dream? Is it a dream that allows some to have "success" as individuals but causes harm to many? Can you pursue this dream while supporting your health in mind, body, and spirit?

Know When to Cut Your Losses

Through the self-discovery process that is the heroine's journey, you might realize you have invested a lot of time, energy, and money into a dream that did not belong to you. It can be devastating when you realize you will never have what you thought you wanted. I know because I have lived it. And I had to give myself time and compassion to grieve, because the loss of a dream is no different from other kinds of losses. What helped me with this process the most was knowing that I was letting go of a dream that was not serving me, so that I could begin discovering and creating a dream that was right for me. That in itself is freeing and empowering.

In finding or pursuing your real dream, as with any good business approach, you learn when to cut your losses and focus instead on new ideas and avenues that may become profitable and successful. For instance, when I found a healthy weight for myself, I simply wasn't big enough to get work as a plus-size model anymore. I evaluated my career, and it was clear to me that I was never going to reach the same level of success that I know I am capable of under the plus-size category. That was when I decided I needed to use the knowledge and skills I'd acquired working in the industry to build success for myself instead of waiting for it to be handed to me.

Since coming to this realization in 2011, I have met and worked with so many different types of people as I built my agency and brand. I have worked with girls as young as 13 up to women in their 30s from all different ethnicities, from different socioeconomic backgrounds, and with completely different body shapes. Some girls begin working right away without much effort because modeling just comes naturally to them, whereas others have to work really hard to get to a professional level—developing their skills, expanding their knowledge of the industry, learning their best angles, and building a strong portfolio. Then there are girls who, no matter how hard they try, can't get the hang of it and will never be working models, even if they look the part.

With modeling, as with any business, you need to learn when to abandon the dream if it is clearly not going to lead to success for you. If you have tried to model for a while and have submitted photos to countless agencies with no response, then as a businessperson you need to realize that this industry is not going to be profitable for you. It is the same for models who do get signed to an agency but don't get hired for work no matter how hard they try or how many photo shoots they do to keep improving their portfolio.

Based on all I have seen and experienced in the industry, in my opinion the goal of being a model should be to make money and use it as a business opportunity, as well as a chance to enjoy its unique benefits. Just remember, even the benefits have their downsides. The most positive parts of the industry for me are traveling and making a good living, yet traveling alone can be isolating and depressing at times. Even when I miss my family and home so much, it is still necessary for me to travel alone in order to work.

For the first several years of building Natural Model Management (NMM) and Healthy Is the New Skinny (HNS), when neither business was making any kind of profit, I supported myself on my modeling money. However, I do see an end for modeling as I am so deeply rooted in the message I am giving you here. When will I quit? Who knows? I think there will come a time when I will just know it is time to let it go, but until then I am still flying solo.

As I shared early in the book, it was when I was feeling lonely on one of my long trips that I started to acknowledge to myself just how unfulfilling modeling was and the negative effect it was having on me. My spirit was languishing, and I wanted something much more meaningful for my life. I would ask myself questions like, "What am I doing to make the world better?" which often led to "What am I doing at all besides showing up to a job and putting on other people's clothes to take photos?" It was a conflicting feeling to realize that, though I had what I had been told I should want, it wasn't what I needed. I had to begin to figure out what it was that I *did* need, and that was the journey I set out on—to reconnect to my true self.

Use Your Inside Knowledge

One way to start to figure out your real dream is to think about what you know. A classic piece of advice for writers is, "Write what you know." I want to tell you, "Dream what you know!" Maybe you have the inside scoop on a particular situation, industry, or societal condition. Such knowledge gives you a head start on any goal you might want to accomplish in that area. In fact, your knowledge may uniquely qualify you to make a real difference in the lives of others.

As the years of my career went by and I became more conscious, the unhealthy nature of the industry bothered me more and more. That's because I know full well that advertising and models are not going anywhere! I could see no end in sight to the damage being done. So, as I found a way to model without compromising my well-being, I wanted to also help other models take their power back and find a healthy way to work within the industry. If I could do it, I knew that others could, too. Ideally, I wanted to change the nature of the industry itself. I am under no illusion about the magnitude of this task. While my efforts have barely put a dent in things, we are gaining momentum.

Once I got a healthy handle on modeling, I didn't want to keep this newfound knowledge and opportunity to myself. I wanted to share it with other girls who were like me. I created NMM so that I could do that. It was important to me to create a community of girls and women who are like-minded in that they realize that by being a model they are putting themselves in the position of being viewed as a role model, and that is a title that comes with responsibility. When that title is placed onto young girls who haven't even had the opportunity to figure out who they are as people, it can cause anxiety.

At NMM, we work to help young models see the bigger picture and to learn what being professional means in the industry. We hold high standards for our models as far as the content they post on social media and how they act on photo shoots and with the crew of these shoots. Being kind and appreciative of opportunities is something we value in our models, and we make sure when girls start drifting from those requirements we get them back on track, or if they are not willing to get back on track, we end our working relationship. The thing that makes us different as a company is that we care. I want to know that each model that I represent well is representing our agency well in return, and that is why it is a partnership.

People often ask me, "Aren't you part of the problem, if you started a modeling agency?" In my perspective, no matter what any of us does for a living and no matter what industry we are in, there is room for improvement. One woman, for example, told me she was a nurse. "Is it fair to say that the medical field has some improving to do? On many differ-ent levels—from patient care, to insurance issues, to medical sales, and so on?" I asked.

"Well, yes, of course," she replied.

"Do you think it is more likely for someone like yourself who has worked in the medical field as a nurse to contribute ideas and feedback that will actually better your industry, or someone like me who has never worked in the industry and knows nothing about it?"

She then understood.

I created a modeling agency because I thought that I could cause a positive ripple effect in the fashion industry by working with girls and women who desired to be mod-els. Instead of treating them as just a product to sell, we treated them as human beings with feelings and emotions. By empowering young models to create a sense of self out-side the fashion industry, encouraging school and outside passions (as most modeling agencies do not), and leading by example and showing them they can do and be more than just a model, I hoped to provide them with options that never occurred to them before.

As I mentioned, in the beginning I started the company to represent myself on my own terms, first and foremost, and then it grew from there. I decided to put my health and well-being first and then see where I got in the modeling world. In essence, by being true to myself and my convictions, I created a way to benefit from all the amazing things that modeling offers—like traveling the world, making really good money, and meeting some amazing people—without having to harm myself to do it. My new understanding gave me the objectivity to evaluate the reality of modeling as a profession; then I was able to start changing the business of modeling from the inside out.

Follow Your Passion

Do you have a "passion project"? You might not even realize it if you do. Is there a particular endeavor that you dedicate yourself to with energy and enthusiasm? You might even lose track of time when you are working on this project because it transports your soul so completely. If you don't have a passion project, could you be denying yourself one? Is there something you have wanted to pursue with all your heart, but you've told yourself that you didn't have the time or that other things were more important? Listen to your heart, please. Your passion project could make a positive impact in your life and in the lives of those around you.

If not for modeling, I may never have had the opportunity to have many wonderful experiences. At the same time, I was detaching from the illusion of what "being a model" was supposed to mean, and separating myself from the negativity the industry harbored. When I began listening much more closely to myself, I was inspired to create something of my own, which is how I started HNS as a body-positive blog and social-media platform to promote messages of healthy body image and self-love. I used income from my modeling jobs to fund my passion project because for the first four years I didn't make a single dollar from it! But I didn't care because making money was not my goal. I was working every day to create a safe and positive community where girls and women could come together, learn from each other, and begin to heal without judgment.

As part of my passion project, I would do photo shoots of girls and share their body-image stories. I used social media to spread the message about our true beauty as women, and as our followers grew, so did my passion. I realized that I was not alone in my efforts, and that inspired me to work harder. That was when I began to speak at schools, and I started connecting personally with young girls and understand the pain they were going through. This was the first time that I started to feel truly of value, and I knew that regardless of whether I earned money at it or not, this was my true passion and purpose—my real dream. This example from my life illustrates an important principle: When you feel *truly* of value, you know you are on the right track. You know you are following, or at least touching on, some aspect of your real dream.

Now, after turning HNS into a brand to help support my ability to create body-positive content and spread the messaging via social media, and developing NMM into the top agency for curve models on the West Coast, I have found success far beyond what modeling has given me. My businesses allow me to travel and make a good living, as modeling has done, but they also fuel my passion to make a positive difference in the lives of girls and women everywhere. That is something modeling alone could never offer me. I still get to take pictures, which I enjoy, but now I get to do it working with my husband as the photographer, and we shoot images that we feel are natural, healthy, *and* beautiful. I no longer have to worry about fitting into someone else's idea of beauty or what I should look like because if a client doesn't like me, that is okay. I have plenty of other things keeping me busy, and I no longer view it as a personal attack or rejection. I now just think, *That wasn't meant for me, but there are good things out there that are.* I get to be my authentic self for my own brand that I created from my passion. It doesn't get any better than that!

If I had known years ago what I know now, I wouldn't have waited so long to try to discover my real dream. If, when I first walked into a modeling agency when I was 17, they had told me, "Katie, you can choose Door Number One, where you will just be a model. Or you can choose Door Number Two, where you will create not one but two businesses that will inspire girls and women to love themselves and allow you to make a great living, work every day with your husband (whom you adore), and travel for fun while furthering your understanding of beauty and life in general. Which door do you choose?" OMG, Door Number Two every time!

Find Your Fit

I'm sure you have heard the expression that you can't fit a square peg into a round hole. Your dream shouldn't be forced. It shouldn't require you to change your essence. It should come as naturally as slipping a round peg into a round hole.

I realize today that I was never meant to be a model. It was never something that brought me joy. And I have never identified with the title of "model" as a crown that sits on my head and brings value or superiority. I never had an easy go in the industry, simply because I never quite fit. My body size didn't fit, my ideas about beauty didn't fit, and my passion for authenticity didn't fit! So I constantly struggled with the idea of needing to be something other than myself in order to be enough. Despite my inner conflict and desire for change, I was also being held back from discovering where I *did* fit by the fear of leaving the only career I had known (at least, the form in which I knew it).

Deep down we all know what we need to do and what is best for us, but it takes time to build the courage to accept, trust, and act on that inner knowing. Deep down I knew that I was not born to just be beautiful. I was born for much more than that. So were you.

Eventually, I reached a point in my consciousness and understanding of my true self where it was time for me to explore the idea of finding a new dream. I had to create something for myself that fit who I was at the core and would not constantly be a force against me that brought negativity and fear into my life. I realize now that a true, authentic dream that is aligned with your true, authentic self brings positivity, inspiration, and feelings of accomplishment and contentment. It has no expiration date, because it is a part of your essence, your innate inner beauty. That is what I desired, and it is what I found as I followed my intuition about what was important to me.

Posing in photos to sell clothing could never give me the fulfillment and joy I now receive from educating and empowering girls and women. No one ever told me that this could be a dream or a career; it was something that unfolded for me by my staying true to myself on my own path of self-discovery. By having the courage to seek something else when I realized that what I thought was my dream was actually unhealthy for me, I found my true calling—the place where I fit in the world.

EXERCISE: ASSESSING YOUR DREAM

It can be difficult to determine whether a dream is authentic to you or you have adopted it from outside sources. This exercise will help you make this distinction, so you are able either to cut your losses on a false dream or pursue your real dream with vigor.

For the following steps, consider only one dream at a time, and repeat this exercise for each dream that you have.

Step 1: Identify one of your dreams as you understand it now. Take a moment to write several sentences about your dream on a piece of paper.

Step 2: Look at the two lists below. Which list holds more *true* statements about your dream?

A	B
I've had my dream from a young age or for as long as I can remember.	I remember when I discovered my dream.
I feel that my dream was created or influenced by other people, such as my family.	I had personal experiences that sparked my interest in my dream.
Following my dream makes me feel insecure.	Following my dream makes me feel fulfilled.
The requirements of my dream make me feel like I'm not enough or I don't have what it takes.	I have the natural abilities and qualities necessary to achieve my dream.
Pursuing my dream causes harm to me physically, mentally, or spiritually.	My dream is making me happier or healthier.
I feel anxious about following my dream.	I feel passionate about following my dream.
My dream makes me feel disconnected from others.	My dream connects me more deeply to others.
When I think about or pursue my dream, I feel as if I am not good enough.	When I think about or pursue my dream, I feel valuable.
My dream is fulfilling someone else's goals for me.	My dream lets me be my authentic self.
My dream serves only myself.	My dream allows me to share my love and gifts with the world.

> If list A includes more statements that are true about your dream, then it is probably a false dream. Please rethink your dedication to this dream; it is not serving you.
>
> If list B includes more statements that are true about your dream, congratulations! It is probably your real dream—perhaps one of many you will pursue in your life.

Choose Instead of Wait to Be Chosen

Every day I choose to model healthy body image and self-love. It is my passion and purpose. No one gave me permission or chose me to do that. You have the opportunity to stop waiting for others to choose you and instead choose yourself!

Girls write to me all the time on social media and say, "You are so inspiring. I hope to one day be like you." I usually respond with, "One day? Why not start today? Only, don't be like me—be *you*."

At any point you can choose to put goodness into the world, and that in itself is inspiring. As you become more connected to your true self, you become less concerned with how others view you. You are then able to be authentic. That doesn't mean you will have life all figured out or there won't be ups and downs; it just means your honesty and authenticity about life in a world of false advertising will be inspiring. I promise. They cannot not be.

■ ■ ■

My purpose is to assist you in reconnecting to your authentic self and true beauty. Then, together, we can challenge the negative view far too many people have of women as a whole—instead of valuing and treasuring us, and seeing us as having the love, goodness, and wisdom that will ultimately save the world. We will achieve this not by tearing ourselves and others down, but by lifting ourselves and one another up. And that is what Part IV of this book is dedicated to.

■ ■ ■ ■ ■

Part Four

HOW YOU CAN HELP HEAL YOUR CORNER OF THE WORLD

Chapter 18

Spreading Your Love

Once you have learned to embrace your true self, love yourself, and live a life that is aligned with your real dreams (the ones that come from you and no one else), it is time to help others do the same! You do this by sharing your love, supporting others in finding and making their way, and otherwise giving your unique gifts to the world. By knowing your truth, speaking your truth, and living your truth, you demonstrate to others that they have permission to find, speak, and live their truths, too. This is what the world needs.

There is no single road to success. Each of our paths will be unique to us and our life purpose. No matter what path we each choose, we can love and support one another along the way and celebrate together at the top as sisters. For women as a whole to be free to live authentic lives that are fulfilling and harmonious in mind, body, and soul, we need to do a few important things first.

Consume Consciously

Stop buying, buying into, or supporting—in any way—messages, brands, or products that don't support you back! That means being conscious of what you invest your time, energy, and money in. The power of advertising lies in the profit. The companies that are making money stay in business and set the trends.

The only way to shift the tide of what is being peddled to women is to purchase brands that offer women something healthy and self-loving and do not sell products or advertising through imagery or messaging that keeps women disempowered and small. Again, it's not consumerism itself that is the enemy here, but rather the manipulation of your subconscious through media messaging and advertising. It's wonderful to consume that which contributes to our well-being and becoming our best selves.

What I have tried to accomplish in writing this book is to give you tools to analyze and examine media and advertising messages. I urge you to ask questions like, "Are they selling me a product that is beneficial to me or that I actually need? Or are they selling me a promise of something their product can never deliver—happiness, acceptance, popularity, and love, which is what we all truly desire?" Then you can consciously decide if you support their advertising—their messaging and imagery—and feel it is healthy for you, for women, and for the world.

You will find that you get quite good at this as you operate more and more from self-love. You'll become a champion for all things nourishing and positive. That will make you much more sensitive to negative energy and able to spot it much more easily than ever before. With this awareness, you can make a healthy choice as to what products, brands, and messages to support. In making decisions this way, you stay aligned with your true self and contribute to the greater good for women as a whole.

Keep in mind that no amount of money, success, fame, status, or beauty will ever fulfill you when you do not like yourself. Although we tend to not believe this, it's absolutely true. No matter what you obtain externally, you will always live with the feeling of never having enough. Therefore, you will spend your life consuming, in hopes of filling that void.

Celebrate and Support Others

We need to stop any and all competition with and comparisons to other people, especially other girls and women. The belief that we must compete arises out of the fear that we ourselves are not enough. But the truth is that we *are* enough.

The number one comparison that needs to go is judging our appearance against that of others. We must see that the idea that we have to look like other people to be happy is simply false. I'll say it again—happiness does not come from our physical bodies! At my heaviest adult weight I was not happy or healthy, but my husband thought I was beautiful. At my lowest adult weight, again I was not happy or healthy, but I was getting compliments from everyone around.

Happiness does not come from your body; it comes from your soul. Enjoying life through your body and its physical health contributes to your well-being and happiness. But health and happiness are not some end-result image—rather, they are a present-moment experience. You do not have to look like the image of health and happiness portrayed in the media to experience the truth of it.

Let me share an example. I posted an image online of myself in a swimsuit from our Body Love Bikini line. The image was not retouched, and I was lying on the couch laughing after a fun day at the beach. The caption read, "Being comfortable in your own skin means accepting yourself when you are alone as well as when you are in the company of others. You know when you are chillin' on the couch in a hoodie or underwear and you couldn't care less about how you look? That is the kind of freedom you can give yourself at all times! Your body has the right to be natural despite the opinions of others, and it feels amazing." I thought it was a really nice post, and it got lots of positive feedback. Then I noticed one comment that said, "Yeah, I would love myself too if I looked like that in a bikini." Do you see how easily we can choose to deny ourselves the right to self-love through comparing ourselves with others? The reality is that my body plays zero role in *you* loving *your* body!

Comparing ourselves never benefits us—it only robs us of our right to self-love. When you are truly happy with yourself, all feelings of envy and jealousy toward others fade away. You can appreciate the beauty and awesomeness of others without feeling threatened. You don't desire to be like other people; you desire to be the best version of yourself. Women who are authentic and happy and who lift others up as they lift themselves up embody an energy that is undeniably beautiful. As you begin to love and accept yourself more, you start to see the difference between physical beauty and true, authentic beauty that shines through a person.

There is no place for envy and jealousy when you are filled with goodness, positivity, and love. So, remember, when those "weeds" pop up in your beautiful garden, spot them, dig them up, and toss them in the trash. It is your job to "tend your garden" and keep negativity out of the positive, loving, nurturing space you have created for yourself.

Now, I know from experience that what I am advocating is challenging. I am by nature an extremely competitive person, and therefore I have had to work really hard on that aspect of my personality. Because although competing pushes me to improve my abilities and skills, it also brings negativity into my intentions and pits me against others. Competing with other girls only creates a divide, when our goal should be to unite. When I find myself feeling competitive, I remember that I need to be collaborative instead. I stop and take time to reconnect to my true self and the task at hand, which is to create a better world not just for myself but for all girls and women. The following exercise illustrates my approach.

EXERCISE: DERAILING COMPETITIVENESS

When you feel yourself becoming competitive with someone else, take time to really reflect on the following statements:

- *I am not better or worse than anyone else; I am just myself.*

- *The task at hand is larger than anything I could ever accomplish on my own, and the message is far more important than my ego.*

- *I can choose to compete with others, which separates us and brings negativity into my life. Or I can choose to be secure in my abilities, my gifts, my purpose, and myself—knowing that when my unique self is combined with other amazing women, our energy will be magnified and become more effective.*

- *I am enough. I have enough. We all can win.*

Consider that love accepts everyone as they are. When we come from a place of love, there is no need to compare ourselves with others or to compete with them. We *are* all love. This is a profoundly peaceful place to be. In the next section, we explore how we can make truly loving contributions to the world.

Put Your Focus on Love

Every person needs to feel like they belong. We all need support and love, and together we can actively look for the true beauty, unique gifts, and enduring spirit in one another and support each other's development!

When we understand that we are deserving of love and the opportunity to become the best version of ourselves, we can then give that gift to others. We can be of service to the world by making others' lives better and spreading love wherever we go. If you think you need to create a company, write a book, or have a million followers in order to do that, you are mistaken. Our contributions come in many forms, shapes, and sizes—but all count. We are here to contribute to the shift in consciousness in our own specialized ways with our unique gifts. Some of us will take on very difficult, large tasks because that is what our spirit chose for us to do. Others provide healing to those in our sphere just by being ourselves. Our energy alone can do that.

Do you see, then, how none of us is more valuable than the next? Because we are all doing the same work, with the same shared goal of embodying our true self, we are all contributing our gifts in the way we are individually the most effective. No competing, only collaborating with love in our hearts and united in our spirit and intent for goodness for the world.

Each day, we must ask ourselves, "How can I love others more?" All of us can contribute love to the world every single day. What are some ways that you can use your energy, gifts, and abilities to spread love? For me, it can be something as small as smiling at others. People sometimes make fun of my husband and me because we know every single person at our local Starbucks and are always saying hello and talking about life. We enjoy people and having an authentic and pleasant exchange with them. We also enjoy when people are negative and not entertained by our positivity, making it our goal to "break" them. We make it a challenge to alleviate their bad mood and see if we can get them to lower the protective wall they have put up to keep others out. Sometimes we are successful and sometimes we are not, but we enjoy the challenge of bringing a smile to every person's face.

When I do presentations at schools, I stay as long as needed to speak with every person who stays after waiting to talk with me. I hug as many people as I can because we all need that human interaction and connection. I take time to connect to the female spirit every day and feel love and gratitude for being born a woman and for understanding my purpose in life. I am so grateful to be alive at this important time in history.

All of these little things I do contribute love to the world. You, too, can take time each day to consciously put love into the world and feel that love in return. We do not need to know one another to love and support each other. For example, the fact that you have read this far in this book means that you and I have made a connection. We have had a positive and loving exchange without ever actually meeting face-to-face. When we can feel ourselves connecting at the level of spirit this way, it becomes evident that we are not just our bodies! We are so, so much more.

Limitless Love and Beauty

An aspect of love that you should always keep in mind is that it is infinite. Take a look at your family. When there is a new baby added to the family, you don't subtract love from others to give to the baby. Your love grows to accommodate all members of your family. Beauty is the same! There are infinite forms of beauty in the world, and one does not subtract from any other. As women we must accept that another woman's beauty does not subtract from our own. We are all beautiful, just in different ways. As I learned this valuable lesson, I began to see other women as allies instead of enemies. Today, I'm happy to say, I have reached a level of self-love and security I never knew possible—where I can look at other women and appreciate both their beauty and my own.

Once you reach that level, too, you will become aware of those who do not have this understanding quite yet. That is okay! When you accept yourself, you can accept others where they are in their own understanding and not take it personally, like the woman who looked at my photo and denied herself the right to love her body because it did not look like mine. I realize that that is her choice, not mine. I understand how she feels and don't judge her for it. Yet I know there is a different choice she could make that will result in her being happier and healthier, and I will hold fast in my encouragement of her to do so. As I do that, I hold the energy and help create the possibility for her to shift. All any of us can do is try to offer guidance and be role models of love and compassion and our own values. We can't actually "save" anyone else. We can only inspire and influence others by being our best.

Our societal programming runs so deep in our thoughts and decision making that we have to allow others the dignity, time, and processes they need to learn, evolve, and grow. And maybe they won't. Either way, your job is to continue to discover your truth, speak your truth, and live your truth. That in itself is the most powerful and inspirational contribution you can give to this world.

Enough Success to Go Around

Like love and beauty, success is also limitless. I love this analogy that my husband brought to my attention: "There is a Home Depot and a Lowe's. They are both home improvement stores, so they sell the same things, and yet they are both successful. Sometimes, they are even across the street from each other!" That always pops into my head, and then I laugh about how silly it was to feel like there was not enough success to go around.

Success is something we all can create; there is no limit to how much we can each have, because success is infinite! For instance, this book could be a bestseller and be hugely successful. Guess what: it could inspire you to write a book that becomes a bestseller and is hugely successful, too. (And I would love to read it and support it!) As my success does not take away from yours, your success does not take away from mine.

Collectively our success only furthers the goal of creating a world that is more positive and loving! It is time for us to realize that we are unique spirits who cannot be copied or replaced. When you live connected to your true self, you have such a strong sense of security in knowing there is only one you and that uniqueness is your power and your gift. We must celebrate and support other women and their amazing accomplishments because they open the door for others to join them! That is how we will lift the oppressive negativity that keeps us small and give ourselves the freedom and strength to rise up together.

■ ■ ■

By following my truth, I've provided girls and women with a path for success that they may have never thought possible. Each time one of us does this—paves her own way and breaks new ground—we give permission to others to create a unique dream of their own. Without knowing it, we model for others—just not in the traditional sense. Through our courage, effort, and success, we inspire others. In Chapter 19, we look at how we can model authenticity, goodness, and love for the world.

■ ■ ■ ■ ■

Chapter 19

Becoming a Role Model

I didn't actually *do* anything to earn the opportunity to be a model. I simply naturally had a look that the industry wanted and was fairly photogenic from the start. I was valued and validated for only one small and superficial aspect of myself—my physical body and appearance—and because of that, I was keenly focused on that aspect, which caused me to be disconnected from a much larger and more meaningful part of myself—my soul and life purpose. The result was anxiety, fear, self-loathing, and depression. Ironically and much to my surprise, despite my success in what I was made to believe I should want, I was caught up in a negative life cycle.

As I've said, I can look back now and understand that I never actually desired to be a model; I wanted to contribute great things to the world. I believed, however, as so many girls and women do, that to do that, I would need to be a model—or at least be beautiful and famous—so that others would want to listen to what I had to say. As prevalent as that belief is today, I now know that it is inaccurate. You might think that my visibility has come by my being a model, but that's not the truth. My platform has been built out of the energy of who I am, my passion for what I believe in and wish to stand for, and the messages that I convey.

All any of us needs to do is embody the qualities we value and "follow our bliss." The things in life that energize our spirit will transform us into the most meaningful kind of model we can be—a role model. Although we might talk about how we "don't like society" and what it does to us, the fact is that *we are society,* so we have to be the ones to change it—again, from the inside out! We do that by first changing ourselves, by—as Gandhi said—being the change we wish to see in the world. We can only do that when we are true to ourselves.

Letting Go of the False to Gain What Is Real

It took me a long time to realize that I was going to have to let my false dream go to obtain what, for me, would be real. It was a tough thing to do if for no other reason than because it was a program that my brain had run on for 10 years. Letting go was scary. I was uncertain and fearful about what would—or wouldn't—come next. For most of us, living in uncertainty is hard. It's natural and normal to want to control our outcomes and destiny, and yet that is impossible when we don't know what that is!

One of the bravest things we can do is to embrace uncertainty, trust that the universe has something wonderful in store for us, then, putting one foot in front of the other, move forward with faith. Again, this can feel challenging—and confusing. When I first realized that modeling was never going to serve my true self and calling in life, I wasn't sure what to do about it. I didn't know what steps to take to find and live my real purpose. I only knew that I wanted to. My best understanding at the time was that my passion had something to do with female empowerment and a focus on body image, but I struggled with what to do with that awareness.

I recall a pivotal moment in my process of letting go of the false so I could pursue my real purpose and dream. One day, during the time frame that I had reached my lowest adult weight and was a size 6, I was lying on the kitchen floor crying after having licked frosting off a baking sheet. My behavior made me realize the depth of my self-loathing and how, in trying to be what others told me was valuable, I had been depriving myself of things that brought me joy. I knew that *this* could not be the real me.

That day led me to have a long talk with my husband, who was so encouraging and inspiring. I told him I just hated the modeling industry and what it does to girls, both within and outside the business. I wanted nothing more to do with it because it was so wrong! I was frustrated and really angry, not only at the entire situation but also at myself for the part I played. After all, I was working and benefiting financially from the industry. He said to me, "If you know that something is wrong here, why would you quit and let them win? Don't quit. Instead, take what you have learned and use it to create something better. You know the truth, so go out and teach it. In doing so, maybe you can help other girls who are struggling, too."

Bradford was right. Even though it might have been easier to just quit and walk away and find something else to do with my life, I knew I had to tell the truth about the industry and shed light on how it was damaging to women and girls. I had to at least try to go against this system that causes so much harm to so many.

I first started where I saw an opportunity, after a mother told me the girls at a Beverly Hills elementary school were not eating lunch. As I spoke to that third-grade class about health and body image, I realized that those girls weren't looking at me and thinking, "Oh man, she is too big to be a model." Nor did they hold the other false ideas about my body that the modeling industry had implanted in my brain. As they looked up at me with big, beautiful eyes and open, impressionable minds, I knew that I could tell them anything I wanted and they would believe me. That day I learned the honor that it is to give a meaningful and honest message to others. By my being present and caring for others' well-being, we collectively had a beautiful experience.

This was a turning point for me. I had never felt that before. I had never experienced 25 third-grade girls come up to me and hug me, and apparently that is exactly what I needed at that time. Some of the girls would tell me stories. One said, "My mom will lay on the bed and say, 'I am so fat!' when she puts her pants on, but I think she is beautiful and not fat at all." Some girls wouldn't say anything but would just hug me. I cried the whole drive home that day because the feelings were so overwhelming.

After having pure, positive intent and unconditional love as my sole focus with them, something permanently changed in me. Gone were the last remaining inklings of wanting to conform to the mold that the modeling industry had provided me. Now I wanted to completely demolish that destructive mold. I realized that I was not going to be fighting back for only myself but also for those girls who had just hugged me so tightly. I realized it was okay to let go of the dream I'd had of modeling, because in doing so I would be allowing myself to fulfill my real destiny—by transforming into what I was meant to be all along.

I decided to take action, and what started as speaking to a small elementary school class turned into a simple blog where I wrote my truth. That simple blog turned into a school program, which turned into a new website to feature others and help them change their lives. That new website turned into an entire brand that sells clothing with a healthy form of advertising, using a variety of body types to create content to spread our body-positive message. That brand has evolved into this book—and it all started with me licking frosting off a baking sheet on the kitchen floor, feeling frustrated, angry, and unfulfilled, and wanting to quit.

Perspective is an amazing thing, isn't it? You cannot worry about where you will end up—all you can do is follow your passion, purpose, and dream now in this moment. Believe me, if you do that, moment by moment, you will be led to right where you are meant to be, where you will contribute to the greater good.

Choosing Authenticity

I have learned that the people we find to be the most inspiring are the ones who are the most authentic—who live as their true selves. As you become more aligned with your truth, you learn how to detect that authenticity in others, and, because of the quality of your own energy, you attract it into your life.

I choose to practice what I preach, and I live my message every day—not because I am trying to gain approval from others but because I genuinely love being myself. I speak my truth and live my life with an open mind and compassion for others. I now understand that when you choose to live without judgment of yourself and others, you see that everyone is the way they are for a good reason. I love to learn about those reasons to better understand how I might contribute to others in a positive way. Likewise, I've learned when to not be around people who want only to subtract from my energy rather than offer a healthy, positive exchange. I love to learn and think in depth about the universe and life as a whole because I always want to strive to be the best version of myself that I can be—connected to my mind, body, and soul. All any of us can ask of ourselves is to strive to be our most authentic and best self.

In fact, it is the *pursuit* of becoming your best self that makes you a game changer, not some imaginary perfect end result! Too often, we believe that we can only be inspiring if we have all the answers. We think we need to have our shit together all the time, but that is false. Every person at every stage in the process of becoming their best self is inspiring. This is a lifelong journey, a process of learning, growing, doing, and being, which we are in until the very end!

Don't get caught up in the idea that being perfect makes you inspiring; this will only slow your progress. Again, it is authenticity—realness—not perfection, that is our goal here. I recognize that this can be hard when we live in a "picture perfect" world, yet there is nothing more important for becoming who you truly are and achieving your real dream. This can be tricky, and it trips a lot of people up.

For example, one model I used to work with had very low self-esteem, yet the messaging she put out into the world through Instagram focused on "loving her curves." As a girl she had been overweight, and, as a young adult, she had a larger build than the other girls with whom she modeled. But she wasn't happy with her body at her healthy, normal weight, so she starved herself to get closer to the skinny beauty ideal. The result was that she became bitter and unhappy and never fully accepted herself, no matter what her weight was. She would post old pictures of herself at her smallest size on Facebook, presenting a false self to the public, hoping for their approval.

That strong desire for outside approval is a symptom of a lack of self-love. This happens all the time on social media! People post photos that do not reflect their true current appearance because they are hoping for approval—or, more accurately, are afraid of not getting it—from others. The problem with this is that when the false image gets positive attention, it increases the person's self-loathing because she is getting validation for what she wishes she was, not what she is. That is not authentic self-love. That is conforming to the idea of how you need to be in order to be inspiring to others.

We have all been guilty of posting the perfect photo with the best angle versus the real moment that maybe wasn't the most flattering. What I have learned is that when you are brave enough to take off the mask of perfection and show the real you, it is immediately inspiring because it is so rare that girls and women get to see and experience that kind of authenticity. I receive more "likes" on social media on a photo showing my natural stomach while in a bikini than I do showing a perfectly posed photo. The reason is that when you live your life according to who you truly are now (rather than who you are striving to be), you give others permission to do the same. And that's something we all want, because it nurtures our soul. When we do that, we become the best kind of models there are—role models.

Role Models Come in All Shapes and Sizes

Because every person is at a different stage of consciousness, there is a need for role models at every phase and level of development. Every girl and woman looks (and is) different, so there is a need for all different types of role models for girls and women to relate to! Why? Because each role model gives other people permission to love who they are and the courage to be themselves and become the best version of themselves. Do you really think the media and fashion industry are going to provide those for us? No way. That is why we must honor our unique purposes and callings and become the role models the world needs—the same role models we missed growing up.

You do not need to be a fashion model or famous to have a profound effect on those around you. Think of people you have known in your day-to-day life who have inspired, encouraged, or supported you in being your best. You, too, will affect others that way—and you will do it via the qualities you embody and the good energy that shines and vibrates through you when you are being your authentic self.

Role Models Aren't Perfect

In this book, I have asked you to let go of the idea that you need to be "picture perfect" to be of value. A similar concept applies to being a role model. We have to let go of the idea that we must be the "best" role model, the "most" inspiring, or fit some kind of role model ideal. The truth is that there is no such thing as a perfect role model (or human being). "Perfect" is not authentic or real.

Furthermore, that way of thinking just brings you back to the competitive and judgmental perspective that tells you there is room for only a select few to be successful. That is false! Every single one of us can be inspiring and successful by living our truth. There is room for all of us to create the life we want as we follow our passion and live our purpose—in fact, nothing would serve the world more.

Role Models Don't Need to Be Famous

There are some incredible women making a profound difference in the lives of others in their corners of the world. Some of these women receive media attention and awards, while others might not be well known and yet are still game changers. Whether they are in the news or not, the many women creating positive change worldwide all share what I like to call a "beautiful warrior" spirit. It's the same spirit that you and I both have.

Right now, I'd like to introduce you to a couple of women that I have met and personally consider role models because of the positive impact they had on my life.

Kami

Kami Craig is an American water polo player who won a silver medal at the 2008 Olympics in Beijing and a gold medal at the London games in 2012. In 2015, she was a member of the U.S. Pan American Women's Water Polo Team.

I met Kami after I reposted one of her images on Healthy Is the New Skinny's Instagram page. In the photo, Kami was with members of the U.S. women's water polo team, holding up the American flag after winning gold at the 2012 Olympics. I was inspired by the body diversity of the female athletes in the photo; it was just beautiful. In that one image you could see health and beauty in multiple sizes and shapes, and so I was really honored to share it.

As Kami and I started to talk, we realized we are a lot alike and each admired what the other does. Both of us grew up with learning disabilities, including dyslexia, and we both have a passion to show that those differences and labels do not define a person or restrict their greatness. When I look at Kami and her unbelievably fit and strong body, she inspires me to be strong. She owns her body, her size, and her strength—and they contribute to her being the best version of herself.

Kami is an authentic person and genuine role model. Although you may not know her name, she is still there every day, kicking a lot of water polo ass and inspiring girls to connect to their own unique greatness.

Tiffany

I met stunt driver Tiffany Susan through a friend and was blown away by her story. Tiffany was involved in a horrible car crash at age 17. As she describes it, "My Volvo was hit by an SUV that ripped through my windshield and down the driver's side of my car, taking my face with it." After 18 surgeries to reconstruct Tiffany's face, she was left with several scars across the left side. I couldn't believe it when she showed me the photo of her accident and then her disfigured face. I had never seen anything like it.

She told me a story about leaving the hospital with stitches covering her face. It just so happened to be around Halloween, and when people would see her in public, they would come up to her and say, "Wow, your costume is so amazing! That looks so scary and real!" She laughed while telling me this story. I was in awe of her profound sense of self. She was an extremely strong spirit and seemed to be unaffected by her scarred face.

When I spoke with her, she told me, "I have never been one to be concerned with my looks. I was more focused on doing the things I loved doing. After the accident, I was just happy to be alive. I wasn't worried about my scars. People come up to me all the time and comment on them, asking me what happened. In a way, I feel I was meant to have these scars to help spread an inspiring message. They belong to me, and I see them as beautiful." Truly, the scars on Tiffany's face are not nearly as noticeable as her incredible energy and her authentic spirit.

Tiffany comes from a family of "mechanics and mudslingers" who "love to get dirty." She had always loved working on cars with her brothers and believed she was just as capable of doing the heavy lifting as any boy. As a way to cope with the trauma of the crash, she tried stunt driving. Today she is a professional stunt driver for feature films and is enjoying success in a male-dominated profession. She is also a driving instructor, mechanic, inspirational speaker, wife, mother, and, most of all, an inspiring human being.

I learned so much about beauty and strength from Tiffany, as well as the importance of gratitude and living in the moment!

■ ■ ■

Kami and Tiffany are the kinds of women I choose to model myself after, not celebrities on red carpets. The image you see of celebrities and models is not representative of the real people. It is the product of a public relations machine. It is not authentic; it is an image that has been created—fabricated—to attain the public's attention for the purpose of making people money. Women like Tiffany and Kami aren't trying to inspire people so they can get a modeling job, movie role, corporate sponsor, or even more followers on social media. They simply *are* inspiring—by being themselves and pursuing what's meaningful to them regardless of who is watching. That is the inherent power we all possess to be influential in our society.

What Qualities Inspire You?

Beneath the inspiration we feel when we look at others are specific qualities—characteristics we admire, value, and, believe it or not, already possess. That is, if we appreciate something about someone else, it means that that same quality is also within us, even if it's dormant or only in seedling form. To become a powerful role model to others, you must first identify the qualities you would like to embody—qualities you value and that truly inspire you. This is how you begin to consciously create who you are and become the role model you have always wanted to be.

I want you to do an exercise here that will assist you in connecting to your inner greatness—to the qualities you would like to develop and strengthen, those that mean the most to you. These same qualities that you find inspiring in others will, as you develop and embody them more and more, be the same ones that others will one day soon also find inspiring in you.

EXERCISE: INSPIRATION FROM A TO Z

1. On a clean piece of notebook paper or in a digital file on your computer or phone, write all the letters of the alphabet—A to Z—down the left side of the page.

2. Next to each letter of the alphabet, write a quality that begins with that letter that you value and that inspires you. The quality should be in adjective form. For example, for the letter

A, you might write "authentic," "altruistic," or "artistic." For the letter B, you might list "brave," "bold," or "beautiful." Do your best to write at least one entry for each letter of the alphabet; feel free to list more. (If you feel stuck, think of people you find inspiring and ponder what qualities about them seem to move you the most.)

3. Once your list feels complete, choose three to five qualities on it that are the most inspiring to you at this moment in time. These are the ones you are going to begin working on. Circle them, and then rewrite them in a separate list.

4. One by one, go through each of these qualities and think about how you can begin to develop or embody it more in your life *right now*. Write down two or three action steps that you think would increase the presence of that quality in you.

5. Take action! Commit to working on developing these qualities. Obviously, this will take some time, but perhaps not as long as you think. When we are intentional and conscious in our choices, results can come quite fast.

Whenever you are satisfied with the level to which you have developed your chosen qualities, do Steps #3 through #5 all over again with new qualities to work on. As you can see, this is a process of self-development and self-improvement that can go on for our entire lives!

■ ■ ■

We all have the power to choose what qualities to embody with every thought we have, every word we speak, and every action we take. It is our small but conscious choices that make up who we are moment by moment and thus who we will have become at the end of the day. This is how we grow into being the best version of ourselves over time. This is how you become the real you, the one that is aligned with your soul and has the greatest potential to impact others.

■ ■ ■ ■ ■

Chapter 20

Girl Gang

If you look around in our society, you see that men have all kinds of ways they rally in support of one another—like the military, sports, and working out, to name a few. They even have the "Bro Code," an etiquette for men to follow. One rule of the code is that male friends should stick together and not abandon each other for relationships with women.

So, what do we as women have? Where are our ways to rally and support one another? Where are the movies that show the story of heroically overcoming all odds to inspire millions and live our dreams or save the world? Oh wait . . . we *have* seen that movie a million times over, but only for men. What about female heroes, warriors, and role models? We are just starting to see the rise of female action heroes like Katniss Everdeen in *The Hunger Games* series (played by Jennifer Lawrence in the film adaptations), a girl who proves herself worthy to lead a rebellion against a cruel and tyrannical regime.

The Hunger Games (the first film in the series) far surpassed industry expectations, with an opening gross of $152.5 million. That seems to be some confirmation of the universal desire to contribute something important to the world. I know *I* don't just want to be pretty; I want to be like Katniss and fight for what is right! I want to be a part of something bigger that will have a profound effect on the future of this planet.

For us to do this, we have to join together. The bond we create as women is not one that is *against* men, but *for* what is healthy for ourselves. It is time that we unite and create a community that is supportive, nonjudgmental, kind, compassionate, loving, and most importantly, all-inclusive. It is time to create our Girl Gang!

Connect in Spirit

Even if we are not able to meet in one place physically, we can be connected through our spirits—through our thoughts and intentions and the feelings in our hearts. Remember our discussion in Chapter 10 on the power of thought and the concept of sympathetic vibration? Our thoughts have the power to connect and heal each one of us. (What we think, we attract.) Our vibration/energy can affect those around us, even those we are not in direct physical contact with.

How do you think we as women might shift if we all were connected to one another through kind, loving, supportive thoughts; compassion; and gratitude for having the same female spirit? For so long we have felt deep pain and sadness in our isolation, thinking we suffered alone. What if that pain and sadness were not just our own as individuals but a collective experience shared by women around the world?

We are continuously connecting through our love and through our pain. And, knowing this, we can consciously choose to send love and encouragement to the collective female energy and spirit that exists in all of us. We can choose to support each other in so many ways, and our thoughts and intentions are extremely powerful tools in doing that.

Join or Create Like-Minded Communities

While we need to connect in consciousness to the female spirit everywhere, we also need to have a local, physical connection through a community of like-minded, supportive, and kind women who genuinely love and support one another. We can do this by healing ourselves, increasing our individual love of self, and then directing that love outward to help other women who are in our sphere of influence. Remember, the task of healing women as a whole—of helping us become free from beliefs that keep us bound and small—is too large to tackle alone; we must join together to be successful in achieving the healthy, happy, authentic lives we were always meant to live. That requires us to take action and create communities for supplying encouragement and assistance where there is a lack of support and love for women.

This is what I have striven to do by creating Natural Model Management, where we have more of a supportive family dynamic than any other modeling agency I have heard of or seen. I support our models as human beings and encourage them to operate from a place of self-love and to contribute positively to the industry and the girls who look up to them. Although I cannot control what each person decides to do, I can create an environment that promotes this goal.

I also built Healthy Is the New Skinny to be a social-media community where we can gather for a common purpose. It has grown into a huge group of girls and women from all over the world who connect every day online, sharing positive affirmations and sending messages of support, love, and self-love into the world. From there, I started a body-image discussion group called Beautiful Warriors, to give girls a place to come and just talk about their body-image issues and secret pain. Actively listening to others is extremely eye-opening and helps to develop our sense of compassion and understanding toward others. We soon realize that we all have a story that matters and we all have experienced pain.

The energy of all three of these venues motivated me to develop our Re-Model Me events. We first do a presentation about media manipulation and body image, which is truly an awakening and a game changer for so many. Then we give girls a chance to participate in a fun, professional photo shoot without hair or makeup teams. The aim is to build their confidence and give them the opportunity to see how truly beautiful they are, as they are, right now. We host events in Los Angeles and travel to schools around the country, teaching students the same tools you have gained from this book.

All of these different elements build a community of like-minded girls and women who are working toward the same goal: self-empowerment and mutual empowerment!

Follow Your Intuition

I was inspired to create these communities after listening to my intuition. I then followed through with action to try to make them real. I was not sure how I would create any of these things (or if anyone would even show up once I did!), but I didn't let that uncertainty stop me. Too often, self-doubt stops us from listening to our inner guidance and following through with the higher calling of our souls. Fortunately, I have reached a point where I trust the guidance of my intuition and have faith in my ability to act on it. I do not always know why I feel the need to do or create something, and I don't have to; I simply trust that there is a reason far bigger than I might, in that moment, understand.

How many times have you wanted to do or create something and then thought, *No one will buy it*, or *No one will show up*, or *No one will care*? The surest way to prove yourself right is to not create anything. After all, people can't care about, join, or support something that doesn't exist!

I was able to connect with women who share my passion because I created something that was in line with my purpose and true self. That energy, intention, and goal attracted others who share the same energy, intention, and goal. Had I never started my businesses or created events and online communities, there would have been no way for all of us to connect. That is why it is so important to take action. You don't need to be sure about it. Just take the first step. And then the next. And then the next. One foot in front of the other, guided by your own inner compass.

Create Our Own Girl Gang

We must boldly take inspiration from all of our sisters in spirit. We must join hands, hearts, and spirits to fight back against the powers that be that wish to bring harm to the female body, mind, and soul. It is time for us to take action and create an invincible Girl Gang of our own!

Don't wait! The time for this is now. We have never needed each other more than we do today! This is our chance to wake up, speak up, and rise up together! It is time to stop being a victim of our society and transform into the beautiful warriors we were born to be. As each of us begins to change individually, our society will change. As we each live our truth, the limited beliefs others have of women will be challenged and proved wrong.

There is strength in numbers. We cannot rise from oppression alone. We need each other. Won't you join us in creating our own Girl Gang? Here are the steps:

1. *Know your truth.* Go on a journey to discover your real beliefs, true beauty, unique gifts, passions, and purpose in life.

2. *Live your truth.* Live every day connected to the real you, which is far more than your physical body. Make choices that are aligned with your purpose, your dream, and the greater good. Let your life itself be your greatest accomplishment.

3. *Speak your truth.* Vocalize how you feel and what you are passionate about. If you know in your heart something is wrong, speak up! Advocate for the things you know are good and healthy. Rally in support of others who are brave enough to take this step. By doing so, we are showing them that they, too, are part of our Girl Gang and, no matter what, we will love and support them.

4. *Take action.* You must take action in order to create something—whether that something is a change in what is or something that is entirely new. When you feel inspiration, you must trust in it, push through the self-doubt, and take action with all your might! Every time one of us creates something true to ourselves, we provide

an example and an opportunity for others that did not exist before.

5. *Create or join a community.* You can take a leadership role and create a community for women to join, such as a workout group, positive body-image group, book club, blog, brand, website, or social-media platform. Or you can find one you love and join it! Anything that gets women connected in positivity and love, with similar interests and goals, is a must.

6. *Generate positivity.* When you find the community where you feel inspired to be your best self, spread the word to others. Healthy Is the New Skinny has a huge membership of girls and women, not because we are always advertising in magazines or on TV but because those who are part of our community genuinely love it. Wherever you find your tribe, share that good news with others. If you see something on social media that you find inspiring, pass it on to others and share why it is inspiring to you.

7. *Avoid negativity.* An important way to protect and enhance your positivity is by avoiding negativity. Know that happiness is uncomfortable for some people. People who don't understand that they have the ability to choose to be happy may try to bring you back down to a darker place. It is true: the more you shine, the more others will try to bring you down with negativity. That is only because they think they have to compete; they do not yet realize that they can shine, too. Do what

you have to do to avoid the negativity vortex. That means unfollowing people and brands on social media that trigger you to have negative thoughts about yourself, ignoring people who have dedicated their lives to being mean and hurtful in person and on the Internet, and avoiding people who want to bring you into the downward spirals that are their everyday lives.

8. *Leave judgments behind you.* If you judge, you cannot truly love. We are allowed to be different and have different beliefs, cultures, bodies, and spirits. Empowerment is not about being one particular way. (That would just be conforming to fit a different ideal!) It is our right to choose for ourselves what is best for us and what we believe while respecting others' right to do the same! We do not have to share the same views to support other women and their well-being. We are all connected in love, so we can support and unconditionally love one another regardless of our differences. Our Girl Gang is all-inclusive to those who share the beautiful warrior spirit.

9. *Be bold.* When you reach an understanding of why you are here, unapologetically *own* it! Fulfilling your purpose is your duty in this life, and that requires you to be bold and fearless as you work to achieve your dreams. Believe me— it will require nothing less. Your purpose may not be something that others understand, and that's okay. Your purpose is not meant for them but for you! Stand tall and boldly move forward, knowing you are right where you need to be, doing what you need to do.

10. *Collaborate.* When you find yourself with a balanced, fulfilled life, contributing to the world via your purpose and your dreams, be sure to collaborate with others who are doing the same. Individually, we could never succeed at the task at hand, but together it is possible. Partner with others who share your passion and audience and who are at the same level of consciousness so that you can support each other and grow together.

11. *Trust.* Trust in yourself to know the truth. You are the only one who knows what is best for you. You are also the only one who can welcome those things into your life. Trust in yourself and your purpos. Trust in your intuition, your inner voice. Trust that you are being guided by a loving energy that is much larger than your own understanding.

12. *Own your existence.* You must own your right to live through the body you have now. Your body is what it is at this present moment. It's okay. You can choose to make changes to improve your health. By doing so, you accept that you are worthy of existing. You must own your right to love and be loved. Own your right to learn and to experience life. Knowing how blessed you are to own your physical body in this life as a woman, join the fight for others to have that same right.

13. *Love like there is no tomorrow—like you have nothing to lose. Love more ardently than you have ever loved before.* The answer to every question

and the solution to every problem is love. Now is the time to love like you have never loved before. With love, there is no putting off until tomorrow. Right here, right now, is all that counts. Connect to your spirit, which you may have not previously been in tune with. Make that connection and let that loving energy run through you and out of you, into the world and all you encounter there.

When we take these steps, we improve ourselves and we improve the lives of every single person living in our society today. When we improve the lives of those living today, we improve the lives of generations to come. If you enjoyed reading this book, then congratulations—you have found a like-minded community. We have been patiently waiting for you, and you have been led right to where you are needed the most. You now have the option to join us and become a member of our Girl Gang!

Join Us!

By joining us, you are accepting that you will no longer allow your mind to be kept small, deprive your body of nutrients, or starve your soul of its joy, happiness, purpose, or love. Together we are choosing to leave those things behind us so that we can transform into the healthiest and strongest versions of ourselves. We are building our power in numbers and in our ability to spread love in the world, and we are building the confidence needed to trust in ourselves. Without you, we are not complete. We need you and your unique gifts because, when combined with our own, everyone's are magnified. That is how we will save ourselves and our world.

I personally cannot just sit by when there are women around the world risking their lives every single day fighting for opportunities that should be basic human rights—like the chance to marry the person they love, rather than a man who buys them or one their family forces them to marry; or the option to go to school and study whatever they desire; or the freedom to work at any profession they choose. These women fight for these rights in hopes to one day be free to consciously create themselves and become the women they were always meant to be!

Those women deserve the rights and opportunities we have now—and so do we. It is up to us to accept this great privilege and become who we were meant to be. Only from that place of personal power can we fight for others who still need it. Only when we have a voice can we speak for those who do not yet have their own.

We must do this because we know the truth. We are not even close to where we need to be as a society when it comes to valuing each human being for their individual purpose and gifts. We must rally in support and love to fight for the truth to be revealed and justice to be granted to all. There is no time for self-doubt, and we cannot worry about what the end result will be. We can only apply our individual greatness in each moment and be willing to share it with the world. That is the kind of army this world needs.

■ ■ ■ ■

Afterword

In the process of researching and writing this book, I've learned so much and grown in so many ways. There have also been many developments in my life and work. The biggest personal change is that Bradford and I have become first-time parents to a daughter, True!

Pregnancy has given me a whole new appreciation for my body that I didn't have before. Each day I learn a little bit more about what it means to live this life as a woman. I am learning that my skin gets looser with age but, at the same time, it also gets thicker. So I care less about what others think of me and more about what *I* think of my own self-image and worth.

Both Healthy Is the New Skinny and Natural Model Management continue to grow rapidly. I have been able to start transitioning my career from modeling to public speaking. In fact, I get to teach the very topics covered in this book! I view this as one of my biggest accomplishments because for so long, I felt that my value in society was defined by my looks and therefore I feared letting go of being a model. By practicing what I preach, I was able to follow my passion, my intuition, and what I believe to be my purpose, which boldly took me in a different direction.

So now I'm juggling my roles as a CEO, a wife, a mother, an author, a speaker, and just being myself! This is all new to me, and I know it won't always be pretty, but I realize that all I can do is my best. I'm looking forward to this new chapter of my life, and I hope that you'll connect with me at Healthy Is the New Skinny to share what the next chapter of *your* life has in store.

I hope that now you understand who you are and what your purpose is, and feel empowered to pursue your dreams. I hope that, in the twilight of our lives, we will be able to look back and be proud of the work we did here. We will feel honored to have been asked to be a part of something larger than ourselves that helped so many. We will feel peaceful, knowing we trained and raised beautiful warriors who helped heal the world. And we will look at each other with a smile, knowing that they never saw it coming from a bunch of girls.

■ ■ ■ ■ ■

Bibliography

Chapter 1: A False Dream

Healthy Is the New Skinny Facebook page. https://www.facebook.com/healthynewskinny.

Healthy Is the New Skinny Instagram. https://www.instagram.com/healthyisthenewskinny.

Natural Model Management (website). http://www.naturalmodelsla.com.

Chapter 2: An Unattainable Ideal

ABC News via Good Morning America. "'Thigh Gap': New Teen Body Obsession?" *ABC News*, March 25, 2013. http://abcnews.go.com/blogs/health/2013/03/25/thigh-gap-new-teen-body-obsession.

Clements, Kirstie. "Former Vogue Editor: The Truth about Size Zero." *The Guardian*, July 5, 2013. http://www.theguardian.com/fashion/2013/jul/05/vogue-truth-size-zero-kirstie-clements.

Del Rosario, Cindy. "The 'Thigh Gap': An Elusive and Dangerous Weight-Loss Trend Fueled by Social Media." *Medical Daily*, October 5, 2013. http://www.medicaldaily.com/thigh-gap-elusive-and-dangerous-weight-loss-trend-fueled-social-media-259071.

Lovett, Edward. "Most Models Meet Criteria for Anorexia, Size 6 Is Plus Size: Magazine." *ABC News*, January 12, 2012. http://abcnews.go.com/blogs/headlines/2012/01/most-models-meet-criteria-for-anorexia-size-6-is-plus-size-magazine.

Mandel, Harold. "Victoria's Secret Supermodel Cameron Russell Attacks the Fashion Industry." *The Examiner*, February 19, 2013. http://www.examiner.com/article/victoria-s-secret-model-cameron-russell-slams-the-modeling-industry.

Mascarelli, Amanda. "Fueled by Social Media, 'Thigh Gap' Focus Can Lure Young Women to Eating Disorders." *The Washington Post*, June 30, 2014. http://www.washingtonpost.com/national/health-science/fueled-by-social-media-thigh-gap-focus-can-lure-young-women-to-eating-disorders/2014/06/30/bca303d2-db9a-11e3-bda1-9b46b2066796_story.html.

Morris, Anne M., and Debra K. Katzman. "The Impact of the Media on Eating Disorders in Children and Adolescents." *Paediatrics & Child Health* 8.5 (2003): 287–289. pmcid: PMC2792687. http://www.ncbi.nlm.nih.gov/pmc/articles/PMC2792687.

Mullender, Rosie. "Why No Woman Should Strive for 'a Perfect Body.'" *Cosmopolitan*, October 13, 2014. http://www.cosmopolitan.co.uk/body/health/a19042/thigh-gap.

O'Connor, Clare. "How American Eagle Is Moving in on Victoria's Secret: Wholesome Bras for Teens." *Forbes*, August 19, 2015. http://www.forbes.com/sites/clareoconnor/2015/08/19/how-american-eagle-is-moving-in-on-victorias-secret-wholesome-bras-for-teens.

Robehmed, Natalie. "The Victoria's Secret Fashion Show: A $50 Million Catwalk." *Forbes*, November 10, 2015. http://www.forbes.com/sites/natalierobehmed/2015/11/10/the-victorias-secret-fashion-show-a-50-million-catwalk.

Trebay, Guy. "Looking Beyond the Runway for Answers on Underweight Models." *The New York Times*, February 6, 2007. http://www.nytimes.com/2007/02/06/fashion/shows/06DIARY.html?_r=0.

"Victoria's Secret Fashion Show CASTING." YouTube video, posted by "HOMBRE1Rules," Jan 16, 2012. https://www.youtube.com/watch?v=ujyZtGugVv4.

Whitworth, Melissa. "Victoria's Secret Show: What Does It Take to Be a Victoria's Secret Angel?" *The Telegraph*, November 7, 2011. http://fashion.telegraph.co.uk/news-features/TMG8872623/Victorias-Secret-show-What-does-it-take-to-be-a-Victorias-Secret-Angel.html.

Willsher, Kim. "France Votes to Ban Ultra-Thin Models in Crackdown on Anorexia." *The Guardian*, April 3, 2015. http://www.theguardian.com/fashion/2015/apr/03/france-bans-skinny-models-crackdown-anorexia.

World Health Organization. "BMI Classification." http://apps.who.int/bmi/index.jsp?introPage=intro_3.html.

Chapter 3: How the Beauty Ideal Brings Us Down

Bahadur, Nina. "Dove 'Real Beauty' Campaign Turns 10: How a Brand Tried to Change the Conversation about Female Beauty." *The Huffington Post*, January 21, 2014, updated February 6, 2014. http://www.huffingtonpost.com/2014/01/21/dove-real-beauty-campaign-turns-10_n_4575940.html.

Celebre, Angela, and Ashley Waggoner Denton. "The Good, the Bad, and the Ugly of the Dove Campaign for Real Beauty." *The Inquisitive Mind*, February 19, 2014. http://www.in-mind.org/article/the-good -the-bad-and-the-ugly-of-the-dove-campaign-for-real-beauty.

Ciambriello, Roo. "How Ads That Empower Women Are Boosting Sales and Bettering the Industry." *Adweek*, October 3, 2014. http://www .adweek.com/news/advertising-branding/how-ads-empower-women -are-boosting-sales-and-bettering-industry-160539.

"Health Consequences of Eating Disorders." The National Eating Disorders Association (NEDA). https://www.nationaleatingdisorders.org/ health-consequences-eating-disorders.

Krupnick, Ellie. "Aerie's Unretouched Ads 'Challenge Supermodel Standards' for Young Women." *The Huffington Post*, January 17, 2014, updated January 25, 2014. http://www.huffingtonpost.com/2014/01/17/ aerie-unretouched-ads-photos_n_4618139.html.

Chapter 4: Desire and the Subconscious: It All Started with a Man Named Freud

Ackerl, Isabella. "Vienna Modernism 1890–1910." Translated by Erika Obermayer. Vienna, Austria: Federal Chancellery, Federal Press Service: 1999. https://www.bka.gv.at/DocView.axd?CobId=5035.

Cowan, Alison Leigh. "Advertising; Ad Clutter: Even in Restrooms Now." *The New York Times*, February 18, 1988. http://www.nytimes. com/1988/02/18/business/advertising-ad-clutter-even-in-restrooms -now.html.

Gibson, Owen. "Shopper's Eye View of Ads that Pass Us by." *The Guardian*, November 19, 2005. http://www.theguardian.com/media/2005/ nov/19/advertising.marketingandpr.

Jones, J. Sydney. "Vienna 1900." J. Sydney Jones (blog). http://www .jsydneyjones.com/vienna1900.html.

McLeod, Saul. "Sigmund Freud." SimplyPsychology. 2013. http://www .simplypsychology.org/Sigmund-Freud.html.

Smith, J. Walker. "The Myth of the 5,000 Ads." Choice Behavior Insights. http://cbi.hhcc.com/writing/the-myth-of-5000-ads.

Thornton, Stephen P. "Sigmund Freud (1856–1939)." Internet Encyclopedia of Philosophy: A Peer-Reviewed Academic Resource. http://www.iep .utm.edu/freud.

Wikipedia, s.v. "Edward Bernays." https://en.wikipedia.org/wiki/ Edward_Bernays.

Chapter 5: Awakening to the Media Manipulation

Christensen, Wendy. "Torches of Freedom: Women and Smoking Propaganda." Sociological Images, The Society Pages, February 27, 2012. http://thesocietypages.org/socimages/2012/02/27/torches-of-freedom-women-and-smoking-propaganda.

Curtis, Adam. *The Century of the Self,* BBC Documentary series.

Petrecca, Laura. "Axe Ads Turn Up the Promise of Sex Appeal." *USA Today,* April 17, 2007. http://usatoday30.usatoday.com/money/advertising/2007-04-17-axe-sell-usat_N.htm.

Time Staff. "Your Doctor Wants You to Smoke." *Time.* Photo essay. http://content.time.com/time/photogallery/0,29307,1848212_1777633,00.html.

Walker, Louise. "Beware the Men (and Women) in White Coats." The Brain Bank North West, April 17, 2012. http://thebrainbank.scienceblog.com/2012/04/17/beware-the-men-and-women-in-white-coats.

Chapter 6: Big Girl in a Skinny World

Tommy Boy. Directed by Peter Segal. Los Angeles, CA: Paramount Pictures, 1995.

Chapter 9: Redefine Beauty

Abba, Agaila. "Big Is So Beautiful in Mauritania that They're Force-Feeding Girls as Young as Five." *Thaqafa Magazine,* July 21, 2014. https://thaqafamagazine.com/2014/07/21/mauritania-force-feeding.

Bosell, Steve. "Thailand's Long Neck People." *Absolute Thai Lifestyle Magazine.* http://www.absolutethai.com/thailand%E2%80%99s-long-neck-people.

Flannery, Russell. "Solitary Woman: Chinese Startup Culture Is a Male-Dominated World." *Forbes,* April 4, 2013. http://www.forbes.com/sites/russellflannery/2013/04/04/solitary-woman.

Foreman, Amanda. "Why Footbinding Persisted in China for a Millennium." *Smithsonian Magazine,* February 2015. http://www.smithsonianmag.com/history/why-footbinding-persisted-china-millennium-180953971.

Gansmiller, Allison and Alex Frantz. "Kayan Tribe." Beauty Across the Globe, January 7, 2012. https://sites.google.com/site/beautyacrosstheglobe/kayan-tribe.

Haworth, Abigail. "Forced to Be Fat." *Marie Claire,* July 20, 2011. http://www.marieclaire.com/politics/news/a3513/forcefeeding-in-mauritania.

Roberts, Jeff. "Why Do So Many Cultures Idolize the Western Caucasian Image of Beauty? A World-Wide Issue That Is Out of Control." Collective Evolution, August 11, 2014. http://www.collective-evolution .com/2014/08/11/why-do-so-many-cultures-idolize-the-western -caucasian-image-of-beauty-a-world-wide-issue-that-is-out-of-control.

Schiavenza, Matt. "The Peculiar History of Foot Binding in China." *The Atlantic*, September 16, 2013. http://www.theatlantic.com/china/ archive/2013/09/the-peculiar-history-of-foot-binding-in-china/279718.

Wedoud, Mohamed Yahya Abdel. "Women Fight Mauritania's Fattening Tradition." *CNN*, October 12, 2010. http://www.cnn.com/2010/WORLD/ africa/10/12/mauritania.force.feed.

Chapter 10: Harness the Power of Your Thoughts

Assaraf, John. "Why You Should Be Aware of Quantum Physics." John Assaraf: Achieve Even More (blog), August 18, 2010. http:// johnassaraf.com/law-of-attraction/why-you-should-be-aware-of -quantum-physics-2.

Atkinson, William W. *Thought Vibration*. Brainy Betty. http://www .brainybetty.com/2007Motivation/William%20Atkinson%20 -%20Thought%20Vibration.pdf, p. 3.

Casey, Susan. "Why Oprah Decided to Start Her OWN Network." Oprah .com, from the January 2011 edition of *O, the Oprah Magazine*. http:// www.oprah.com/spirit/Oprah-Winfrey-Network-Sneak-Preview.

"Dr. Jill Bolte Taylor," the website of Dr. Jill Bolte Taylor. http://www .drjilltaylor.com.

"Einstein Explains the Equivalence of Energy and Matter." AIP Center for History of Physics. https://www.aip.org/history/exhibits/einstein/ voice1.htm.

Kehoe, John. "Mind Power Basics." Mind Power with John Kehoe. http:// www.learnmindpower.com/using_mindpower/basics.

Lejuwaan, Jordan. "Emoto's Water Experiment: The Power of Thoughts." HighExistence. http://www.highexistence.com/water-experiment.

Loken, Camillo. "The Law of Vibration." One Mind—One Energy: The Power Is Within. http://www.one-mind-one-energy.com/ Law-of-vibration.html.

Walia, Arjun. "Nothing Is Solid & Everything Is Energy – Scientists Explain the World of Quantum Physics." Collective Evolution, September 27, 2014. http://www.collective-evolution.com/2014/09/27/this-is-the -world-of-quantum-physics-nothing-is-solid-and-everything-is-energy.

Webmaster, All4NaturalHealth.com. "Health Quotes, Inspiration and Motivation." All4NaturalHealth.com. http://www.all4naturalhealth.com/ health-quotes.html.

"What Is the Photograph of Frozen Water Crystals?" Office Masaru Emoto. http://www.masaru-emoto.net/english/water-crystal.html.

Wikipedia, s.v. "Sympathetic Resonance." https://en.wikipedia.org/wiki/Sympathetic_resonance.

Chapter 12: Make Healthy the New "Skinny"

ABC News Staff. "100 Million Dieters, $20 Billion: The Weight-Loss Industry by the Numbers." *ABC News*, May 8, 2012. http://abcnews .go.com/Health/100-million-dieters-20-billion-weight-loss -industry/story?id=16297197.

Levy, Jenna. "U.S. Obesity Rate Inches Up to 27.7% in 2014." Gallup, January 26, 2015. http://www.gallup.com/poll/181271/obesity -rate-inches-2014.aspx.

Chapter 13: Create Great Health

Merriam-Webster Online, s.v. "health." http://www.merriam-webster.com/ dictionary/beauty.

Chapter 14: Discovering Your True Self

Cummings, E. E. "A Poet's Advice to Students." In *E. E. Cummings: A Miscellany*, edited by George J. Firmage, pg. 13. New York: The Argophile Press, 1958.

Rumi, Jalal ad-Din. Quoted in Wayne W. Dyer, *The Power of Intention* (Carlsbad, CA: Hay House, 2010).

Runaway Bride. Directed by Garry Marshall. Los Angeles, CA: Paramount Pictures, 1999.

Chapter 16: Discovering Your Purpose

Goodwin, Jenifer. "Rate of Eating Disorders in Kids Keeps Rising." *U.S. News & World Report*, November 29, 2010. http://health.usnews.com/ health-news/family-health/brain-and-behavior/articles/2010/11/29/ rate-of-eating-disorders-in-kids-keeps-rising.

Park, James. *New Ways of Loving: How Authenticity Transforms Relationships*, 6th ed, pg. 132–33. Minneapolis, MN: www.existentialbooks.com, 2007. Quoted in: http://www.tc.umn.edu/~parkx032/NWL132.html.

Chapter 19: Becoming a Role Model

Associated Press. "U.S. Women Win 1st Gold in Olympic Water Polo." *Komo News*, August 9, 2012. http://www.komonews.com/sports/US-women-win-1st-gold-in-Olympic-water-polo-165643506.html.

Smith, James. "USA Water Polo Announces 2015 U.S. Pan American Teams – USAWP." Total Waterpolo, June 23, 2015. http://www.totalwaterpolo.com/2015/06/23/usa-water-polo-announces-2015-u-s-pan-american-teams-usawp.

"Tiffany Susan," the website of Tiffany Susan. http://tiffanysusan.com.

Wikipedia, s.v. "Kami Craig." https://en.wikipedia.org/wiki/Kami_Craig.

Chapter 20: Girl Gang

Baumeister, Roy F. "The Meaning of Life." *Aeon*, September 16, 2013. https://aeon.co/essays/what-is-better-a-happy-life-or-a-meaningful-one.

Canal, Emily. "'Insurgent,' 'The Hunger Games' and the Rise of the Female Action Hero." *Forbes*, March 18, 2015. http://www.forbes.com/sites/emilycanal/2015/03/18/insurgent-the-hunger-games-and-the-rise-of-the-female-action-hero.

Wikipedia, s.v. "Bro Code." https://en.wikipedia.org/wiki/Bro_Code.

Young, John. "Box Office Report: 'The Hunger Games' Posts Third-Best Opening Weekend Ever with $155 Mil." *Entertainment Weekly*, March 25, 2012. http://www.ew.com/article/2012/03/25/box-office-report-hunger-games.

Acknowledgments

I would like to thank my mother, Janice White, and my editor, Brookes Nohlgren, for working with me on this book. Writing has always been a challenge for me due to my learning disabilities with language and struggles with dyslexia. I don't know if I would have been able to get this book finished without your constant encouragement, support, and hard work in editing. I couldn't be happier with the outcome, and I am grateful for this experience with you both.

I want to say thank you to my amazing husband, Bradford, for always believing in me. Not only did you listen to me read each chapter of this book out loud multiple times, but also you genuinely acted like you were listening each time! And that is why I love you. You have always loved me for who I am and that love alone changed the way I viewed the world. You make me laugh every single day, and you truly inspire me to be a better person. I love you.

True, I am so grateful you chose us to be your parents. We can't wait to show you the world.

■ ■ ■ ■ ■

About the Author

Katie H. Willcox is the founder and CEO of Natural Model Management and Healthy Is the New Skinny (HNS). Using her 13 years of experience in the modeling industry, Willcox strives to change the game of body image by giving people the tools to challenge the beauty ideal implemented by the media.

Founded in 2011, HNS is a brand that promotes positive body image and lifestyles for women all over the world. HNS has been featured in a variety of publications, including Fox News, *People* magazine, and the *New York Post*. In addition, HNS has been heralded as one of the top social-media pages to follow for body positivity, according to MTV and *Marie Claire*.

Using HNS as her platform, Willcox speaks out against harmful advertising and encourages people from all over the world to model healthy body image. As a public speaker, Willcox aims to educate, inform, and empower girls and women to rise up against media manipulation and teaches them how to protect against it.

Join the movement! Visit www.HealthyIsTheNewSkinny.com and follow us on Instagram @healthyisthenewskinny.

■ ■ ■ ■ ■

We hope you enjoyed this Hay House book. If you'd like to receive our online catalog featuring additional information on Hay House books and products, or if you'd like to find out more about the Hay Foundation, please contact:

Hay House, Inc., P.O. Box 5100, Carlsbad, CA 92018-5100
(760) 431-7695 or (800) 654-5126
(760) 431-6948 (fax) or (800) 650-5115 (fax)
www.hayhouse.com® • www.hayfoundation.org

■ ■ ■

Published and distributed in Australia by: Hay House Australia Pty. Ltd.,
18/36 Ralph St., Alexandria NSW 2015
Phone: 612-9669-4299 • *Fax:* 612-9669-4144 • www.hayhouse.com.au

Published and distributed in the United Kingdom by: Hay House UK, Ltd.,
Astley House, 33 Notting Hill Gate, London W11 3JQ
Phone: 44-20-3675-2450 • *Fax:* 44-20-3675-2451 • www.hayhouse.co.uk

Published and distributed in the Republic of South Africa by:
Hay House SA (Pty), Ltd., P.O. Box 990, Witkoppen 2068
info@hayhouse.co.za • www.hayhouse.co.za

Published in India by: Hay House Publishers India,
Muskaan Complex, Plot No. 3, B-2, Vasant Kunj, New Delhi 110 070
Phone: 91-11-4176-1620 • *Fax:* 91-11-4176-1630 • www.hayhouse.co.in

Distributed in Canada by: Raincoast Books,
2440 Viking Way, Richmond, B.C. V6V 1N2
Phone: 1-800-663-5714 • *Fax:* 1-800-565-3770 • www.raincoast.com

■ ■ ■

Take Your Soul on a Vacation

Visit www.HealYourLife.com® to regroup, recharge,
and reconnect with your own magnificence.
Featuring blogs, mind-body-spirit news, and
life-changing wisdom from Louise Hay and friends.

Visit www.HealYourLife.com today!